Cyber Weapons of Mass Psychological Destruction:

And the People Who Use Them

Author
Dr. Vikram Sethi

With a forward by
Dr. Terry Oroszi

Greylander Press

Cyber Weapons of Mass Psychological Destruction:
And the People Who Use Them

ISBN   978-1-7348188-0-2

DEDICATION

This book is dedicated to my family, friends, and all those who have supported me in my personal life and professional work.

ACKNOWLEDGMENT

A large part of the research for this book was conducted during my professional development leave from Wright State University, and I am grateful for this support. A large number of colleagues in the cyber world who work daily in anonymity to secure our way of life are an inspiration – especially you, HVN!

A special thanks to a dear friend, colleague, and fellow researcher – Terry Oroszi – for her ground-breaking work under the rubric of "weapons of mass psychological destruction" which inspired me to think creatively and hopefully place the cyber threat in an appropriate perspective.

Table of Contents

TABLE OF FIGURES

FOREWORD

I coined the term, "weapons of mass psychological destruction" (WMPD) in 2015 to include the psychological torture involved in using weapons of mass destruction. The specific definition of WMPD was destructive devices designed to cause death, serious bodily injury, or intense psychological harm through the release, dissemination, or impact of chemical, biological, radiological, nuclear, or explosive (CBRNE) agents. My intent was to emphasize that every terrorist attack reaches beyond the immediate physical damage it causes and into the psychology of its target population, gripping them with anxiety over the potential for personal loss. In this book, Dr. Vikram Sethi has expanded that concept into the cyber world.

Dr. Sethi first came onto my radar when he was directing the Institute of Defense Studies and Education (IDSE). He was the first person I reached out to as coeditor of Weapons of Mass Psychological Destruction (Preager, 2016) in order to take advantage of his skill at breaking difficult concepts down into easily understood language. Another of his talents that I wanted to tap was his versatility: business is his core, but he has an in depth understanding of many tangents, such as homeland security, terrorism, supply chain during a crisis, and of course, cyber. There is rarely a week that goes by without my reaching out to him regarding anything crisis related.

In this book, Dr. Sethi traces the growth of cyber weapons from simple annoyances like Mellissa, to the largely destructive Stuxnet, and hacking from The Impact Team to Guccifer, WikiLeaks, and misinformation campaigns. Sethi asserts that cyber-attacks impose a similar psychological impact as strikes that use traditional weapons of mass destruction. Indeed, cyber weapons are also WMPD, and their use around the world is expanding. This book will help readers distinguish the "real" details from "fake news," and understand the intricate and fascinating realm of cyber warfare.

Dr. Terry Oroszi

Terrorism and Crisis Researcher

in the Field of Homeland Security

PREFACE

This book shows unequivocally that cyber intrusions create deep psychological harm to society – these effects can be so long-lasting and intense that they create paranoia and cognitive confusion. Drs. Larry James and Terry Oroszi[1] proposed the use of the general term "weapons of mass psychological destruction" (WMPD) to describe "acts/tools which have the potential to cause long-term, intense psychological harm to the masses" (p. 8). In their brilliant articulation of this term, we find the genesis of the concept of cyber weapons.

Cyber weapons range from simple ransomware (even though no ransomware is truly simple) to sophisticated bots that can be used to bring down a nation's infrastructure, power lines, banking networks, and even nuclear facilities. The use of cyber weapons to sow seeds of discord in society, change human behavior, and exploit individual beliefs by creating disinformation campaigns has become the new landscape of war and the weapon of choice used by terrorist organizations. This book explores how this is happening in our society today and why these tools are virulent and effective in their use.

---

1   Larry C. James & Terry L. Oroszi, "Weapons of Mass Psychological Destruction and the People Who Use Them," Prager Press, 2016.

There are no books on the market that deal specifically with cyber weapons in the context of psychological impacts and effects, and explore the world of technology from the reference frame of WMPD – the power of cyber weapons to create "hyperreality" in society and build forces of societal disruption which far exceed the harm caused by traditional weapons.

This book brings together current cases of cyber intrusions (1996-2018) and provide the reader with an understanding of their societal impact. I will also show that cyber-attacks have morphed into tools deployed by nation states. My assessment will bring together the fields of technology, psychology, and discourse analysis/semiotics. It will also provide guidance and policy on prevention of the use of cyberweapons. The book includes a discussion of the growth of cyber weapons and examine the primary actors involved in their use. I will also examine international policy issues that are important in this debate and the notion of cyber deterrence.

The "Cyber Weapons of Mass Psychological Destruction and the People Who Use Them" consists of five sections, described below.

Section I: The Road From Cyber Experiments To Cyber Warfare examines the evolution of cyber weapons. I will discuss how the nature of cyber intrusions has changed since the 1990s. What began with a simple "cyber virus," today is reported in the everyday media using terms such as "cyber weapon" and "cyber war." The blast radius of cyber weapons has grown from a single individual to society at large. I will provide a new examination and understanding of the psychological effects of cyber WMPD's as tactical and strategic weapons.

Section II: The Many Ways To Perpetrate Psychological Harm focuses on seven specific cases in recent history which show the trajectory of the growth of cyber weapons. The transition of cyber experimentation to global cyber weapons did not happen at once. I will trace this growth with specific examples to show the sophistication of the perpetrators and the adaptation of weapons to cause harm at a larger scale.

Section III: And The People Who Use Them assists the reader in their understanding of the primary actions who use cyber weapons and their motivations. Three nation states - Russia, North Korea, Iran and their cyber capabilities will be discussed. Each country has its own agenda for the use of cyber weapons, and I will investigate their motivations. In addition, there are individual actors who practice the art of cyber terrorism solely to show off their technical power and prove to themselves that "they can do it." Individual actors are studied and described.

Section IV: Technological Connectedness cover the topic of how technological growth has made it easier for cyber terrorists to reach their goal. Our society is entrenched in a technology growth and use cycle – build goods and services through technologies which speak to one another and use each other's capabilities to provide a seamless experience to the user. In this quest, we find some of the reasons why cyber terrorists are so successful in exploiting the edges of technologies to gain access to systems and create havoc. I also offer advice to individuals and communities to protect themselves against such intrusions.

Section V: Future Considerations covers emerging trends in the prevention and management of cyber weapons. It examines existing global cyber policies and regimes that are in place and how to strengthen them.

SECTION I:

The Road From Cyber Experiments To Cyber Warfare

Chapter 1: We're Not in (Cyber) Kansas Anymore

Chapter One

We're Not in (Cyber) Kansas Anymore

People have been at war with each other since the dawn of time. As the world and its wars have evolved, so has its weapons. The prophecy after the Second World War that the Third World War would be fought with the help of computers seems to be coming true; a cyber war is well underway.

We are in and will continue to be in a perpetual and unrelenting cyber-attack - from nation states and hostile groups (organized and unorganized) to malicious individuals, and even those who simply wish to demonstrate their technical superiority and talent. Cyber-attacks are not just about stealing data and information; they serve to create chaos in our society and confusion in our lives, and successfully turn our stable and mundane everyday life upside down into one of worry, panic, and hysteria. In so doing, cyber-attacks and break-ins become weapons of mass psychological destruction. Never before has the world seen such weaponizing of cyber intrusions at the scale which is evident right now.

On January 14, 2018, 8:07 am, for 38 terrifying minutes, the island of Hawaii reeled under a scare when an emergency alert warning was issued in error, and for thousands of people, the fear of living under the threat of a North Korean missile attack became almost real. Despite the fact that it was nothing more than a false alarm, it caused massive chaos throughout the archipelago in the Central Pacific. The Emergency Management Agency in Hawaii later announced it was a mere human error. As per the daily test routine, a staff member accidentally pressed the "live alert" button instead of "test alert."

A message was sent to cellphones and through the airwaves: "Ballistic Missile Threat Inbound in Hawaii! Seek Immediate Shelter! This Is Not A Drill!" People panicked as if a ballistic missile was indeed headed in their direction. The error was spotted within four minutes, but the terror it spawned lasted 24 additional minutes.

This could well have been a catastrophic event – a nuclear war could have kicked off within a matter of minutes simply because of an error. If the U.S. had taken the error as a serious threat and responded, it could have easily triggered a war between two countries.

The employee, who had worked for the Hawaii Emergency Management Agency for 10 years, sent the missile alert to cell phones across the state by picking the wrong option on his computer for a routine drill and then confirming his choice. People are people, and they did what they might naturally be expected to do in such terrifying circumstances. They flooded roadways, crowded into concrete structures, or ran to police stations. One family hid in a steel shipping container. Others knelt in churches and began to pray. One couple retired to their bedroom, exchanged vows of love, and waited for the inevitable or whatever was coming. Consider for a moment the prospect of waking up to an alarm on the streets about an impending missile attack, gathering one's senses to what action to take, and, worse still, not being able to make any telephone call because the cell phone network is choked with traffic.

What would you do?

The missile scare set off mass hysteria and panic amongst a population that may continue to live under this imagined threat, though such a threat has not been real since 1941! Honolulu police released 24 calls at the request of the local media as representative of the approximately 2,000+ calls placed to dispatchers during the crisis. These span the range of emotions from fear to anger.

"The whole family, all scared, you know?"

"Was that a typo? A really, bad typo?"

"Somebody needs to get their a—whooped!"

Perhaps, what is more telling of the emotion of people and their families is better represented in tweets which were also released:

"Just in case. We love you guys."

"We love you..."

"Please pray we will get inside in time."

"Praying right now."

"I love you all."

"Honey take shelter. I love you."

"I don't know where it is headed but take care."

It is certain that these reactions continued well beyond the four minutes of the actual incident. Many psychological studies show that individuals who are exposed to "fear events" carry those memories over their life, memories that give rise to narratives of constructed reality that can scar lives forever. Will a normal weather alarm dredge up memories of a missile attack later in life? Will it cause irrational fear?

The incident also highlighted a critical weakness in the country's national infrastructure. What if the alarm was set off by a cyber intrusion instead of a human error? The possibility of the Third World War being fought with the help of computers seems nearer than ever before.

Hackers and cyber intruders have successfully penetrated national and local alarm systems before. On April 10, 2017, 11:42 pm CDT, all 156 emergency sirens in Dallas, Texas, went off for 90 minutes. It was not until 1:17 am that engineers finally managed to manually shut off the sirens. This act was perpetrated by cyber intruders, and it resulted in thousands of fear-stricken people calling 911 to ask what could have caused all 156 emergency sirens to go off at once in the middle of the night. A spokeswoman for the city stated in a telephonic interview that the sirens, typically used to alert residents of severe weather conditions and other natural disasters, were misconstrued as a warning of a missile or bomb within the city. Not only the mainstream press but even social media was flooded by users complaining about the system failure in the city. Despite the unrest caused by the cyber intrusion, officials were reluctant to share full details regarding the breach that had caused a wave of fear among Dallas residents.

Both incidents should serve to inform us that our technical infrastructure designed to bring important and key services to us, can be used rather maliciously to do psychological harm to a wide group of people by altering reality. In the process, making us think we are under attack by missiles when there is nothing in sight; waking us up to an imminent threat of a tornado when there is none; and impelling us into action because we believe a certain condition is looming large over us. All of this is conjured up by somebody who succeeded in manipulating our technological infrastructure for malicious purposes. Cyber intrusions have evolved over time. Their application to mass attacks with huge social implications is a stark example of their rapidly evolving sophistication and use by determined individuals and groups, no matter who they are and whatever be their goals and ambitions.

Computer intrusions have evolved hand in hand with hackers' experience and intents. Looking back at the evolution of computer threats, we can spot three cybergenres, which I term as:

1. Cyber annoyances

2. Cyber mafia, and

3. Cyber warfare.

All three differ in terms of their behavior, their attack motivations (as much as we can extrapolate them), and the harm they cause.

In the very first generation of cyber threats are viruses such as "Melissa." This virus was developed by David L. Smith in 1999 and named after an exotic dancer in Florida. It started with the upload of a Word document to the "alt.sex" Usenet group. If downloaded and opened, the virus resulted in shutting down safeguards of Microsoft programs such as Word or Excel. It also had an immense effect on security settings, because Melissa disabled macro security along with spreading itself through infected documents attached with the emails sent to the victims' computer. The damage caused by the virus reached the tune of $1.2 billion and it hit hundreds of websites, disabling hundreds of thousands of people from accessing their email address within six hours of deploying the virus. Despite causing a colossal loss, the creator was fined $5,000 only, along with 20 months imprisonment.

In the broader stream of virus intrusions, Melissa was an annoyance. In fact, when Smith was sentenced, he claimed he had no idea that the virus would have such a devastating impact and inflict the kind of damage it did. He had apparently designed the virus to cause minimal financial damage and meant it to be a non-serious program.

Similarly, "Nimda" appeared in September 2001, a week after the 9/11 terror attacks in the U.S. Nimda, actually "Admin" spelt backwards, was declared a terrorist attack and topped the list of fatal viruses within 22 minutes of deployment. It was considered capable of impacting more than two million systems in a span of 24 hours, with web servers being the primary target. The virus was fatal enough to infect users in several ways such as emails, local networks, and drive-by downloads on websites, vulnerabilities in Microsoft web servers, as well as loopholes created by other computer worms. It allowed the attackers to gain the same access to the system as the users of the system, which meant if the user enjoyed admin-level privileges, so did the hacker. Nimda executed itself to the roots of the hard drive's partition "C," "D," and "E" respectively, besides replicating itself in any folder where it found documents with ".doc" or ".eml" extensions. In the end, the economic damage caused by the virus was upwards of $635 million. The malicious program didn't spare even the Florida Federal Court, which was reduced to operating using paper copies after their systems were infected.

Approximately in 2000, the world of computer intrusions shifted both technically and functionally from mere annoyances to profit motives and extortion. This signaled the dawn of the "cyber mafia." No longer were attacks simply with the aim of inflicting harm or to show off technical superiority, they had larger designs woven around them such as how to hold computer systems and infrastructure to ransom for financial gain.

The "CryptoLocker Ransomware" made its appearance in 2013. This virus consisted of a "Trojan" virus capable of affecting every single system running Microsoft Windows. Set off on May 5, 2013, the ransomware continued to operate until 2014. The sole purpose of this intrusion was to penetrate the security of the system and steal a victim's information. Furthermore, it displayed a message warning the victim to pay a certain sum before a deadline or have their critical data either erased or leaked over the internet. The operatives behind CryptoLocker were demanding and receiving ransom, not only along traditional payment channels but also in the form of cryptocurrency (mostly bitcoins). A rough estimate of the money extorted put the heist at over $3 million.

In the light of the attacks mentioned so far, we can conclude that viruses can cause catastrophic aftermath if deployed effectively and with deadly cunning. Millions or even billions of dollars could be lost in these attacks while countless users might end up being victimized. In later chapters, I will discuss attacks which led to data pilferage from large organizations, such as Sony Pictures, Equifax, and others.

The third generation of cyber intrusions is far darker and more sinister and is not simply related to disrupting and sending emails or holding data for money. The larger design here is the disruption of society and throwing the democratic process into turmoil.

The summer of 2010 saw a severe cyber intrusion when the Stuxnet computer worm "crawled" its way into the systems running Iran's nuclear processing facilities. Having penetrated the system, the worm started replicating itself. While the primary target was the Windows-based Siemens Step 7 software used to protect industrial systems, the malware is believed to have waded through various systems. With the capability to replicate itself, the worm gained access to the facility's logic controllers and devastated over

984 uranium-enriching centrifuges. By some accounts, Stuxnet was a spectacular military success; there were no explosions, no fatalities, no military strikes and yet it pushed back Iran's nuclear weapon program by as much as two years.

In 2014, security researchers uncovered a Stuxnet-like malware, "Havex," programmed to infect industrial control system software of SCADA systems and armed with the power to possibly disable hydroelectric dams, overload nuclear power plants, and even shut down a country's power grid with a single keystroke.

Using this malware, a Russian group of hackers, widely known as "Energetic Bear," successfully compromised over 1,000 European and North American energy firms. Dragonfly, a sophisticated attack group which U.S. sources claim is Russia-based, uses the same techniques to target energy supplier organizations in the U.S. and several other countries.

A blog post published by security firm Symantec described how the Dragonfly group targeted petroleum pipeline operators, electricity firms, and other industrial control systems (ICS) in nearly 84 countries during its 18-month campaign. Most victims were located in the U.S., Spain, France, Italy, Germany, Turkey, and Poland.

Dragonfly reappeared in March 2018 in its "Dragonfly 2.0" avatar, and this time a U.S. CERT advisory suggested that a joint analysis by the Department of Homeland Security (DHS) and Federal Bureau of Investigation (FBI) had found evidence that Russia was actively targeting critical infrastructure in the U.S. The advisory paid particular attention to the indicators of compromise (IOCs) – tell-tale forensic evidence that a cyber-attack has taken place – and technical details of hacker techniques in order to help grid operators limit their exposure to such risks. In astonishing detail, the U.S. government described the extent of the preparation to which cyber groups have gone to develop their understanding of how to penetrate key facilities in the U.S. and other countries such that they could "turn out the lights at will."

SECTION II:

The Many Ways to Perpetrate Psychological Harm

Chapter Two

A Stripper Named Mellissa

Melissa was born on March 26, 1999 on *Alt.sex*,[1] an online newsgroup. It began life as a Word document, which contained purported passwords to several pornographic websites. It was reportedly named after an exotic dancer in Florida named Melissa. Once opened, the virus in the document forwarded itself to the first 50 contacts in the user's Microsoft Outlook contact list.

These first 50 users started to receive email messages with a subject line that read, *"Important Message from ...."* followed by the name of the previous victim; a text message that said, *"Here is that document you asked for....don't show anyone else;"* and an attachment

---

1   Chris Taylor, William Dowell, & Elaine Shannon, "How They Caught Him," Time, 4/12/1999, 153 (14), p. 66

called list.doc, with the same list of user names and passwords. Since the message appeared to come from an acquaintance, it encouraged recipients to open the attachment and continue the chain reaction.

The virus also infected Word templates, so any new document that was created would automatically be infected by Melissa. If these documents were emailed to any user, the infection spread further.

The virus was also corrupting the documents in the system in a big way. If the infection on a computer occurred when the current number of minutes past the hour matched the day of the month (e.g., 9:27 am on March 27), the virus would insert the phrase *"twenty-two, plus triple-word-score, plus fifty points for using all my letters. The game's over. I'm outta here..."* The phrase was actually a reference to one of the episodes of *"The Simpsons"* cartoon.

Melissa was one of the world's first successful email-aware viruses. It forced several large firms to shut their email gateways to control the virus. March 26, 1999 happened to be a Friday, and much of the damage was controlled because of the weekend. Several reports presented at the hearings on Melissa before the U.S. House of Representatives Committee on Science in April 1999 gave examples of affected companies, such as a 500-employee advertising firm that received 32,000 messages in 45 minutes.

The organizations affected included Boeing, Lockheed Martin, and the U.S. Marines. Melissa[2] infected 1.2 million computers and 53,000 servers at 7,800 North American companies that had at least 200

---

2   Lee Garber, "Melissa Virus Creates a New Type of Threat," Computer, June, 1999, p. 16.

PCs. Clean-up efforts are estimated to have costed $561 million!

One of the redeeming aspects of Melissa was that it took only about 20 minutes to develop a pattern to recognize the virus and easily fix it. The flip side of an "easy" virus was that it was effortless for others to replicate it, and variants of it, such as *Papa*, *Cow*, *Marauder*, and *Sundicate*, were quickly introduced.

The search for the Melissa "writer" was dramatic. A virus detector noted that Melissa originated from the email *skyroket.com*. Richard Smith, head of Phar Lap Software in Cambridge, explored other viruses posted from the same email address. Fredrik Bjork, a computer science student in Sweden, suggested that Melissa's code was similar to the work of VicodinES, a virus writer. Richard Smith and Rishi Khan, a nineteen-year-old University of Delaware undergrad, downloaded several files from Vicodin's website and discovered one name embedded in the code thrice – David L. Smith.

AOL soon confirmed that the email *skyroket@aol. com* belonged to Scott Steinmetz but discovered that the account had been highjacked by a New Jersey user. Eventually, the NJ account was tracked back to a phone number belonging to David L. Smith, who was arrested at his brother's house – and all of this happened within seven days from the release of the Melissa virus.

While a formal connection between the pseudonym *ViacodinES* and David Smith was never established, there was more in common between them than differences. David Smith worked as an AT&T contractor and had moved back to New Jersey from Florida after a personal bankruptcy and the loss of an IT job.

The last media mention of David Smith, in The

New York Times, said he was working at the Rutgers University Foundation while on bail as an IT support person and resigned on December 3, 1999 after his court appearance, where he was sentenced to twenty months in jail and a fine of $5,000. After his discharge from prison, he started assisting the FBI in catching hackers.

A motive for why David Smith created Melissa has never been established. A rhetorical analysis by Best & Lewis[3] inferred that incidents like Melissa demonstrate two inherent cultures, which influence such attacks – one which rejects its subversive intent and the other which celebrates it. They further noted that the Melissa virus was followed a month later by the Chernobyl virus that erased hard drives of thousands of computers around the world and was set to strike on the thirteenth anniversary of the 1986 nuclear disaster in Chernobyl.

But they continue to question – what is the end game? What is the culture which induces normal people to create and disseminate such software? Is it truly an experiment gone wild, or is it a desire to sow anarchy and confusion as a means to gain fame?

United States Office of Personnel Management (OPM)

Matthew Dean and Catherine Heddige's (2015)[4] shocking report headlined "China Reportedly Compiling a *Facebook* of U.S. Government Employees," said the personal data stolen over the span of several

---

3   Best, K. and Lewis, J. (2000) Hacking the democratic mainframe: The Melissa virus and transgressive computing. Media International Australia, 95 . pp. 207-226.

4   Matthew Dean & Catherine Herridge, "China reportedly compiling a 'Facebook' of U.S. government employees," http://www.foxnews.com/politics/2015/09/15/chinas-facebook-us-government-employees.html.

high-profile U.S. cyber breaches is being indexed by China's intelligence service into a massive Facebook-like network.

This headline points not only to the data loss from across the federal government but also from private organizations who are federal contractors and hold similar data. Stolen data sources for this index are from the U.S. Office of Personnel Management (OPM) and other intrusions such as the Anthem, Blue Cross, Blue Shield health insurance networks.

Two hackers in 2015 were able to steal data on nearly 21.5 million U.S. federal employees from the database of OPM. So extensive was the damage caused by this loss that Joel Brenner, former NSA Senior Counsel, is quoted as saying,[5]

> *"This is crown jewels material... a gold mine for a foreign intelligence service; and while, this is not the end of American human intelligence, it is a significant blow."*

The FBI director at the time, James Comey, said about the breach,[6]

> *"My SF-86 lists every place I've lived since I was 18, every foreign travel I've ever taken, all of my family, their addresses. So, it's not just my identity that's affected. I've got siblings. I've got five kids. All of that is in there."*

---

5   David Auerbach, "House Oversight Committee Blames Former OPM Leadership For Largest U.S. Government Data Breach In History;" The OPM Breach Is a Catastrophe; June 16, 2015;   https://slate.com/technology/2015/06/opm-hack-its-a-catastrophe-heres-how-the-government-can-stop-the-next-one.html
6   Ibid

The OPM data breach happened over several years and brought up many questions as to why it went undetected for as long as it did. The House Committee6 report ended with 13 specific recommendations about how to avoid similar data breaches and painstakingly described how it happened.

The sequence of events in the data breach is, perhaps, a more interesting insight into how hackers cunningly go about their work in plain sight.

The OPM hack is actually a story of two hackers, reported as $X1$ and $X2$, and is also a story which came to define Advanced Persistent Threat (APT) hacking. Such an attack is focused on high-value assets and stealing data over time. The objective is to maintain persistent presence on the target network, learn as much a possible about the target environment, and steal data over time.

OPM first learned something was wrong on its network on March 20, 2014, when the United States Computer Emergency Readiness Team (US-CERT) notified the agency of data being exfiltrated from its network. OPM then worked with US-CERT to implement a strategy to watch and monitor the attacker's ($X1$) movements to gather counterintelligence. However, unbeknownst to OPM and US-CERT, a second hacker ($X2$) posed as an employee of an OPM contractor (key point) and used the contractor's OPM credentials to log into the OPM system, install malware, and create a backdoor to the network.

As the agency monitored Hacker $X1$'s movements through the network, it noticed hacker $X1$ was getting dangerously close to the background information on employee security clearance. OPM, in conjunction with the Department of Homeland Security (DHS), quickly developed a remediation plan – *"the Big Bang,"* to kick Hacker *X1* out of its system. The decision to execute the plan was made after OPM observed the attacker load keystroke logging malware onto the workstations of several database administrators.

At the time, the agency was confident the planned remediation effort on May 27, 2014, eliminated Hacker *X1*'s foothold on their systems. But hacker *X2*, who had successfully established a foothold on OPM's systems and had avoided detection, remained in OPM's systems post-Big Bang. On June 5, malware was successfully installed on a key point web server. After that, *X2* moved around OPM's system until July 29, 2014, when the intruders registered a domain *opmlearning.org* to use it as a command-and-control center to manage their malware operations.

Beginning in July through August 2014, hacker *X2* exfiltrated security clearance background investigation files. In December 2014, another 4.2 million personnel records were exfiltrated.

On March 3, 2015, a domain, *wdc-news-post.com* was registered by the attackers and used as a command-and-control network. On March 26, 2015, the intruders began stealing fingerprint data. The stolen information included detailed files and personal background reports on more than 21.5 million individuals and fingerprint data on 5.6 million of them.

There are two significant characteristics of the OPM hack:

1. The length of time the two attacks lasted

2. The type and volume of data stolen and its significance

The first known access to OPM's network was in July 2012, and on September 23, 2015, OPM updated its original estimate of the number of data points stolen. The story of the breach, of course, does not end there. In August 2017, the FBI arrested a Chinese national related to the OPM breach, and this will be discussed in a later chapter.

The American Federation of Government Employees[7] claimed in a lawsuit against the OPM that the hackers stole all personnel data for every federal employee, every federal retiree, and about one million former federal employees. This data is thought to include every affected person's social security number, military record, veteran status, address, date of birth, job and pay history, health insurance, life insurance, pension information, age, gender, race, union status, and more.

In addition, OPM reported that 5.6 million fingerprints were stolen. Hackers also got access to SF-85, SF-85P, and SF-86 questionnaires used for background checks. These questionnaires collect sensitive personal information about a person's mental and emotional health, illegal drug use, alcohol abuse, personal finances, police records, involvement in non-criminal court actions, divorces and association with organizations advocating violence. These records include not only information about actual and prospective government employees, but also on contractors and consultants.

---

7 "Federal Union Says OPM Data Breach Hit Every Single Federal Employee," Forbes, June 11, 2015, https://www.forbes.com/sites/katevinton/2015/06/11/federal-union-says-opm-data-breach-hit-every-single-federal-employee/#4da83ba816d2

Information is gathered not only about workers seeking security clearance, but also about their friends, spouses, and family members. It can include potentially sensitive information about the applicant's interactions with foreign nationals – information that could be used against those nationals in their home country. Security clearance background reports often include extremely sensitive information, such as whether applicants had consulted a health care professional regarding an emotional or mental health condition; illegally used any drugs or controlled substances; and experienced financial problems due to gambling.

The Washington Post reported that the CIA ended up pulling out a number of officers from its Beijing embassy in the wake of the OPM breach, mainly because the data leaked in the intrusion would have let the Chinese government know which State Department employees stationed there were not listed in the background check data stolen from the OPM and were working as CIA agents.[8]

HarrisOnSecurity magazine noted that it had started to hear from sources in the U.S. intelligence community that :[9]

> *"If the attackers could steal all of this sensitive data and go undetected for so long, could they not also have granted security clearances to people who not only didn't actually warrant them, but who might have been recruited in advance to work for the attackers?"*

---

8   https://www.washingtonpost.com/world/national-security/cia-pulled-officers-from-beijing-after-breach-of-federal-personnel-records/2015/09/29/1f78943c-66d1-11e5-9ef3-fde182507eac_story.html?utm_term=.64da8eefaf24

9   https://krebsonsecurity.com/2016/09/congressional-report-slams-opm-on-data-breach/

Another element of the data breach came in an unexpected manner on June 16, 2015, when the OPM Chief Information Officer Donna Seymour acknowledged that the information compromised in the data breach included SF-86 data as well as clearance adjudication information. [10]

Adjudication data is far more comprehensive and important than data contained in the SF-86 forms. Data ranges from information on sexual behavior that *"reflects lack of discretion or judgment"* to evidence of *"foreign influence,"* including a broad definition of *"risk of foreign exploitation"* associated with mere *"contact with a foreign family member."*

For instance, information collected to adjudicate a simple *Top Secret* single-scope background investigation includes a *Personal Subject Interview* and interviews with neighbors, employers, educators, references and spouses/cohabitants. It also includes a check of law enforcement records where the individual lived, worked, or went to school in the past 10 years; information that is not included on a standard SF-86.

Certain types of security clearances also require the individual to pass a polygraph examination, which can be extraordinarily intrusive and far exceed the subject matter of an SF-86. Former U.S. officials reported that polygraphers had asked if they had ever practiced bestiality, and what contacts they had with journalists, including socially.[11] All of the data collected during a

---

10 Homeland Security Today, "Breach of OPM Employee Records Raise More National Security Concerns, Officials Say," https://www.hstoday.us/channels/federal-state-local/breach-of-opm-employee-records-raise-more-national-security-concerns-officials-say/

11 https://www.thedailybeast.com/hackers-stole-secrets-of-us-government-workers-sex-lives

polygraph is part of the adjudication data set.

What this means is that the information known to the hackers may potentially comprise all data collected during the initial clearance process and every comprehensive mandatory update, including all of the data from multiple polygraph examinations.

The hackers, thus, could blackmail any employee into becoming a double agent. They could also reach out to senior American officials whose personnel files contain damaging secrets and attempt to extort them or influence U.S. policy.

As John Davis posted on his blog:[12]

> "*Blackmailing is probably the most dastardly type of social engineering there is. Here you are; nice family, good job, couple of kids, respected in the community – life is sweet! Then all of a sudden, someone contacts you and threatens to release some scurrilous information to the public if you don't do as they say. Maybe you were arrested for something embarrassing such as being caught as a Peeping Tom. Maybe it's an embarrassing medical condition such as a venereal disease. Whatever it may be, suddenly you are faced with the choice of cooperating with criminals and breaking the law or abject ignominy – what would you do?*"

Given the extent of information loss, we need to consider what would happen if such a large amount of data were effectively used to cause widespread societal chaos and panic. Hacks like this can readily become weapons of mass psychological destruction.

---

12 https://stateofsecurity.com/?p=3728

Case Study One

Robert Tappan Morris: Hacking's Enfant Terrible

On the morning of Thursday, November 3, 1988, users of the Internet, which, at that point, was a network connecting researchers, developers and engineers at various universities, government institutions, industrial research establishments, and large corporations, predominantly in North America, woke up to find that a malware computer program, "worm," had sneaked into their network the previous night and was rapidly infecting one computer after another. At 8:00 pm EST, November 2, 1988, the worm attacked MIT's PREP computer, a rather insecure machine retired by the research university in 1989, believed to be its first point of penetration.

On the U.S. west coast, the worm struck computers at the policy think-tank Rand Corporation in Santa Monica at 9:24 pm EST, November 2, 1988. After dinner, at around 10 pm EST, when Phil Lapsley and fellow computer science student Kurt Pires, at UC Berkeley, logged into the computer system at the student-run lab in Cory Hall, they happened to notice that "someone" had been making repeated attempts to stealthily gain access to their machine from another computer the way *"a thief would search a house for an open window."* Since the number of attempted break-ins to the machine was way more than was humanly possible, the duo inferred that a computer program was at work.

The two students alerted the software manager for computer systems support, and over the next two days, the Computer Systems Research Group (CSRG) at the university, along with students and staff at UC Berkeley, set to work, developing fixes to destroy the worm on infected computers and to prevent any reinfection. By late evening on November 2, 1988, teams at both UC Berkeley and MIT had *"captured"* copies of the program and disassembled it back to its source form to understand the effect of the infection.

By 5:00 am EST, November 3, 1988, in under 12 hours from the first sighting of the worm at UC Berkeley, CSRG had put on the table an interim set of steps to prevent the worm from spreading. Apart from providing initial updates and fixes to the *"sendmail"* agent, CSRG counselled users to rename one or both of the C compilers and loaders to disallow their usage. These suggestions were posted on Usenet, but by then many of the intended recipients at other institutions had disconnected their systems from the internet to quarantine the worm. Soon researchers at Purdue University, University of Utah, and MIT's Project Athena had also joined the nationwide effort to dissect the worm and suggest timely remedies. By about 7:00 pm EST, November 3, 1988, Purdue had hit upon an effective method to prevent infection by stopping the worm from cloning itself and without any need to rename system utilities. By 10:00 pm EST the same day, CSRG had distributed software fixes nationwide to cure all infections, including for the finger-daemon attack.

The computer worm spread like wildfire across the U.S., infecting 6,000 computers at research centers, universities, and military installations. It brought the internet to a grinding halt by exploiting vulnerabilities in applications closely associated with the UNIX operating system 4.3BSD, developed by CSRG at UC Berkeley, and distributed free of cost to many institutions in the U.S. Derivatives of 4.3 BSD, particularly those running on SUN microsystems computers.

UC Berkeley, by putting just around 20 people to work on the worm through the nights of November 2-3, 1988, was able to not only keep its systems running without a hitch but also broadcast remedial measures across the networks for the benefit of other institutions. However, not everyone was lucky as UC Berkeley. Cornell University, for instance, didn't know it was affected until the wee hours of the morning on November 3, 1988 and unplugged itself from the internet to stop the worm spreading not until late that evening. By November 4, 1988, the internet was pretty much back to normal, though hundreds of systems administrators were still working to clear the mess.

Initial media speculation was that the northeastern

U.S. was the source of the worm proved. However, CNN in its late-night news on November 4, 1988 reported that the author of the worm (and New York Times confirmed the following morning) was Robert Tappan Morris, 23, a computer science graduate student at Cornell and *"brilliant son"* of Robert Morris, *"one of the government's most respected computer security experts."*

Early Life

Robert Tappan Morris was born in 1965 to Robert Morris and Anne Farlow Morris. The senior Morris, a computer scientist at Bell Labs, helped design Multics, an early operating system delivered in 1967, and UNIX operating system. He later became the chief scientist at the government's National Computer Security Center, an arm of the National Security Agency (NSA) responsible for conducting research and setting standards for classified government computers and networks.

Young Morris grew up in the Millington section of Long Hill Township, New Jersey, and graduated from Delbarton School in 1983. He attended Harvard University, where, for two years, he knew Dr. Andrew Sudduth, a staff member at the Aiken Computational Laboratory at Harvard (himself a talented hacker but better known as a world-class rower who was part of the silver-medal-winning U.S. team at the 1984 Olympics). On and off, Morris had worked for Sudduth's lab, often free of cost. The two stayed in touch for several months after Morris had left Harvard.

As a Harvard undergrad, interestingly, Morris appears to have been more concerned about protecting against abuse of computers rather than breaching them. A Cornell University commission would later on find that at Harvard, Morris was a bright student who was bored by routine homework and often devoted his main energies elsewhere.[13] He apparently continued this pattern at Cornell, where he arrived in the fall 1988 for graduate studies in computer science. His Cornell peers said Morris didn't develop many friends in the two months between his arrival on campus and the release of the worm at 7:26 p.m. EST on November 2, 1988.

The worm is believed to have been created over a two-week period. There is no evidence to suggest that anyone from the Cornell community (faculty, students, or staff) aided Morris or knew of the worm before its release. Morris, however, inform one student earlier that he had discovered certain security weaknesses in UNIX. Forensic evidence would later reveal that Morris started using Cornell computers to develop the worm around October 15, 1988. Five days later, Morris made a 300-mile trek to Harvard, staying there with friends for two days. On his return, Morris added code to change the design of the worm significantly to include the *"Method-S"* form of attack, which was capable of exploiting a third vulnerability, a flaw in the *"SENDMAIL"* program used to send emails. It is quite likely that Morris got clued up about this vulnerability during his Harvard trip.

Harvard staff interviewed later by the Cornell University commission, including Sudduth, pooh-

---

13 Ted Eisenberg, David Gries, Juris Hartmanis, Don Holcomb, M. Stuart Lynn, Thomas Santoro; "The Computer Worm: A Report to the Provost of Cornell University on an Investigation Conducted by The Commission of Preliminary Enquirey." February 6, 1989; p. 37

poohed any notion that they might have held a conversation with Morris around the subject of the worm. At the same time, on October 26, 1988, there was an interesting email that went from Paul Graham, a computer science graduate at Harvard and staff member at Aiken Computational Laboratory at the university, to Morris, in which he enquired – *"Any news on the brilliant project?"* Years later, Graham and Morris would become longtime collaborators, setting up Viaweb (1995); Y Combinator (2005); and Arc programming language (2008).

On October 28, 1988, around 7:00 pm EST, Morris reportedly told another student, Dawson Dean, that two years earlier, he had figured out the *"Method-F"* form of attack, which exploited a feature of UNIX (BSD) that enabled a user to obtain certain information about another user on a remote computer. Morris would speak confidently about his knack for cracking into UNIX, according to Michael Hopcroft, another officemate. According to Sudduth, on November 2, 1988, about 11:00 pm EST, he was having a conversation with Paul Graham, and Morris reportedly called Graham and spoke with him, after which Graham told Sudduth that *"something big was up [at Morris' end]."* Sudduth persuaded Graham to say more about the issue, whereupon, Graham confided that Morris had released a virus [sic] which had overwhelmed computers at Cornell and was probably causing much consternation for those connected to the internet.

Sudduth sent Morris an email asking him to call. Morris called Sudduth about 11:30 pm EST but he chose to leave the conversation dangling at places, maybe intentionally or maybe he was in blind panic by then. Morris told Sudduth that *"something was going on,"* without mentioning his involvement in it; though, by now, Sudduth had drawn that conclusion. Sudduth, for his part, gave Morris advice on how to stay anonymous. Around the same time, Dawson Dean reported seeing Morris seated before one of the office computers and he was on the telephone; Dean could pick out words like *"Harvard"* and *"MIT."*

At 2:30 am on November 3, 1988, Morris rang up Sudduth and said in a tone, which suggested he was worrying about something, that he wanted an apology to be relayed across the internet, along with some advice on how to stop the worm from spreading. Sudduth assured him that he would find some way to send out an anonymous message, which he did at about 3:30 am on November 3, 1988. It was too little too late, since Sudduth's message went over email along an obscure route and reached users with a 24-hour delay, by which time, the worm would have devastated more machines, and in any case, UC Berkeley and others had shared many antidotes with the user community. Between November 2 and 6, 1988, Morris repeatedly called Graham, and, at one point, Graham told Sudduth that Morris had used MIT's PREP computer to release the worm.

On November 4, 1988, about 9:30 pm Dennis Meredith of the Cornell News Service received a call from the Washington Post daily. The caller informed Meredith that the New York Times daily was to carry a story the following morning naming Cornell's graduate student Robert Tappan Morris as the perpetrator of the worm. On November 5, 1988, the day Morris made headlines in the national press, Sudduth sent out another message, this time acknowledging that he was the author of the earlier message of apology while still withholding Morris' identity. In November 1988, Cornell formed a commission, comprising faculty and staff picked from various streams like IT, law, computer science, physics as well as the office of the university counsel, to conduct a preliminary enquiry.

Evidence Collected by the Cornell Commission

The Cornell University commission based its findings largely on the trove of data contained in the backup tapes (maintained by the computer science department) of the computer accounts that Morris maintained on two workstations. Dr. Dean Krafft, computer science facilities manager, helped the commission decrypt these backup files. Among other things, these backup files contained a *"complete"* and an *"almost complete,"* October 15 version of the worm, apart from an unencrypted source code version. Other pivotal pieces of evidence included: a) a file containing user ID and password combinations of accounts, including at Cornell; b) a file containing a list of passwords, which were similar to the passwords in the aforementioned file, as well as a list of passwords contained in the worm, and c) a record of Morris' email communication with Graham and Sudduth on November 2-3, 1988.

Telephone records pertaining to the use of the telephone in Morris' office represented another piece of crucial evidence. Interviews conducted by the campus judicial administrator, Tom McCormick, and the chairperson of the commission, M. Stuart Lynn, were another rich load of evidence. Some of the people interviewed where, a) seven students who shared an office with Morris, including Dawson Dean and Michael Hopcroft; b) Samir Khuller, a graduate student in charge of orientation of new graduate students; c) Dr.

Dean Krafft, computer science facilities manager; e) several former and serving staff members and students of Harvard who were acquainted with Morris, including Sudduth; f) Glen Adams of MIT who was officially responsible for the PREP computer, which Morris used to release the worm; g) and staff of UC Berkeley who had been involved in developing patches for the worm. Graham couldn't be contacted by the commission despite repeatedly trying, and the commission observed:

> *"This is unfortunate in view of the role he [Graham] apparently played on the night of November 2 as described by Mr. Sudduth and in view of other light he may have been able to shed on the matter."* Eisenberg, *et al.*, p. 15

Morris chose not to be interviewed by the commission.

The commission's key findings

The Cornell inquiry concluded that Robert Tappan Morris created the worm and released it into the internet. The creation and release of the worm was a violation of the computer science department's computer usage policy. Samir Khuller told the commission that Morris was not present at the first day of his orientation, and probably on the second or third day, he collected the computer usage policy from Khuller. On the following day, Morris skipped Dean Krafft's talk, which was part of the orientation and covered computer security matters. In any case, Morris was or should have been familiar with Harvard's policy on misuse of computer systems. Therefore, the commission felt that Morris knew the acts he committed were wrongful by the standards of the professional community.

There is no direct evidence to suggest that Morris intended for the worm to replicate uncontrollably. However, he would have known or should have known of such a consequence. The uncontrollable replication of the worm clogged the memories of infected computers and eventually brought them to a halt. However, the worm did NOT destroy any system or data. There was no evidence that any of Cornell's faculty, students or staff had assisted Morris in creating the worm or had prior knowledge of the worm before its launch. However, given its technical sophistication, the worm could have been created by many students at Cornell or at other institutions.

Many members of the UNIX community are in two minds about reporting security flaws in UNIX, for fear that publicizing them would open the door to black hat hackers for exploitation before the flaws could be patched in all UNIX versions. Sudduth told the commission that the thought of reporting flaws to UC Berkeley never came to his mind. Scott Bradner of the Harvard Psychology Department Computer-based laboratory, who had supervised Morris during his freshman years, told the commission that the *"Method-F"* flaw was discovered several years earlier by Dan Lanciani, Morris' successor at the lab. The knowledge was widely shared across Harvard and fixes applied in time to most UNIX computers there. Interestingly, no one thought of reporting the same flaw back to UC Berkeley.

Commission Comments

"The act of propagating the worms was fundamentally a juvenile act that ignored potential consequences... Contrary to the impression given in many media reports, the

*commission does not regard this as a heroic event that pointed up the weaknesses of operating systems... This was not a simple act of trespass analogous to wandering through someone's locked house without permission but with no intent to cause damage. A more apt analogy would be the driving of a cart on a rainy day through most houses in a neighborhood. The driver may have navigated carefully and broken no china but it should have been obvious to the driver that the mud on tires would soil the carpets and that the owners would later have to clean up the mess... Experiments of this kind should be carried out under controlled conditions in an isolated environment."*Eisenberg, et al., pp. 7 - 8

First Ever Conviction Under the Computer Fraud and Abuse Act

Morris was suspended from Cornell in 1989 on the basis of the commission's findings, but the college board said Morris could apply for readmission later. The Federal Bureau of Investigation (FBI) was conducting a preliminary investigation to ascertain whether the Morris worm had caused any harm, which would have violated the Computer Fraud and Abuse Act (CFAA) passed by U.S. Congress in 1986. The law made it a federal crime to knowingly access a computer operated by the U.S. government and certain financial institutions without proper authorization as well as disrupt its normal functions. On January 6, 1989, the associate general counsel of Cornell and a member of the commission received a letter from Morris' attorney, Thomas A. Guidoboni, which confirmed that federal investigation of Morris' potential criminal conduct had begun in earnest:

"As you are well aware, the United States attorney for the Northern district of New York has been pursuing a grand jury investigation into the same computer virus incident [that the commission is looking at] and Mr. Morris' involvement therein. The eventual outcome of this process could be a multiple count federal felony indictment against Mr. Morris, and thereafter, a trial on this indictment... Therefore, regretfully, we must decline Cornell's request for an interview at this time." Eisenberg, *et al.*, Appendix II

On November 5, 1988, FBI spokesperson, Mickey Drake was quoted by New York Times as saying that the bureau had *"no history of prosecution in this area,"* under the CFAA (1986). Under the act, a first-time offender is liable to a fine of $5,000 and twice the value obtained in the violation or the loss caused by it. Press reports put the number of infected computers at 6,000, a figure they had arrived at by extending the number of infected computers at MIT to the entire number of computers hooked to the network, assuming that the trend at MIT would hold good for the entire internet.

On July 26, 1989, Robert Tappan Morris was indicted on charges of violating United States Code Title 18 (18 U.S.C. § 1030) of CFAA (1986), becoming the first person to be charged under this act. In December 1990, he was sentenced by the U.S. District Court for the Northern District of New York to three years of probation, 400 hours of community service, and a fine of $10,050, plus the costs of his supervision. Importantly, Morris didn't get any jail time. He appealed, but the motion was rejected in March 1991.

Arguments that Morris used at various times

during the trial were that a) the computer he used to release the worm was not a *"protected computer;"* b) Cornell had given him access to computers and that, his act of releasing the worm was not completely unauthorized either; c) the government failed to prove that he had intentionally altered, damaged, or destroyed computerized data belonging to another; d) the district court had not provided a definition of terms like *"authorization"* to the jury; e) his motive was to demonstrate the inadequacies of security measures on computer networks by exploiting the security defects he had discovered; and f) due to a design error, the worm had replicated itself far more rapidly than he had planned.

The jury found the government's interpretation of the statute with respect to concepts like *"protected computer," "unauthorized access,"* and *"intentionally causing damage,"* more convincing than Morris' defense. Justice Department attorney Ellen Meltzer told jurors there was no question Morris created the worm and sent it out over the national network with the intent of gaining unauthorized access to federal computers. *"Each and every one of you must understand that the worm was not merely a mistake,"* Meltzer said. *"It was a crime against the government of the United States."* [14]

The court reasoned that Morris' worm had gone beyond a mere interdepartmental trespass to affect U.S. government departments, including military research facilities, thus attracting penalties under 18 U.S.C. 1030. Morris' contention that the district court did not instruct the jury on the meaning of *"authorization"* (to

---

14 John Markoff, "Computer Intruder is Found Guilty;" The New York Times; 1/23/2019, p. 21.

access a computer) got short shrift from the jury, which agreed with the lower court that this was a common usage that did not need to be defined.

Life after the worm

Morris completed his sentence in 1994 and cofounded Viaweb in 1998 with Paul Graham. He earned a PhD from Harvard University in 1999 in Scalable TCP Congestion Control, and in 2006, he became a tenured faculty at MIT, where he has been making significant contributions in areas like computer, wireless networking, and operating systems.

Chapter Three

Stuxnet & Flame

This chapter is centrally focused on highlighting the first use of cyber weapons to attack physical facilities. There have been several cyber intrusions before the Stuxnet computer worm, but it is appropriate to label this as the first of its kind. The previous intrusions were mostly centered on networks and servers. Aiming at a physical facility *"unintentionally"* was something new. This chapter will elaborate the two cyber intrusions *"Stuxnet"* and *"Flame,"* which targeted Iran's nuclear facilities.

Stuxnet

Viruses[15] were not, so much, destructive, back in the 1990s: they were just pranks by hackers in order to

---

15 https://spectrum.ieee.org/telecom/security/the-real-story-of-stuxnet

gain access to a system or litter an AOL homepage with graffiti. Now that interlinked networks link countries much more tightly, an attack on a single installation or a country might carry an impact way beyond its borders.

Stuxnet, which first caught the attention of cyber researchers in June 2010, was nothing more than a 500-kilobyte computer worm, though toxic enough to take out centrifuges – almost 1,000 of them – at Iran's uranium enrichment facility *"unintentionally."* It succeeded in infecting nearly 13 other industrial sites within Iran. What is particularly scary about this virus is its ability to replicate and spread on its own. So much so, that unlike other viruses, it can roll out the contagion over a computer network without having to rely on an unwitting victim, lacking any knowledge of the malware, to install it.

The cyber-attack carried out by Stuxnet happened in three different stages. The first targeted Microsoft Windows machines and networks as they were vulnerable enough for it to infiltrate. In stage two, the worm took aim at the Siemens Step 7 software, a popular Windows-based SCADA system responsible for controlling plants and machinery. Arguably, the software is easy to victimize, and yet here is a software that has seen wide deployment in industrial control systems responsible for operating high-tech and critical equipment such as centrifuges. The third stage in Stuxnet's game plan was the attack itself. It targeted and took down the logic controllers that can be programmed to control the spinning speed of the centrifuges. The authors of Stuxnet originally intended the worm to spy on the industrial system, but it was reported that the virus lost control and ended up altering the speed at which the centrifuges spin. It either slowed down their rotational speed or made them spin too fast, and in the process, destroyed them relentlessly.

Even during the course of the attack, Stuxnet spread itself so stealthily that it would become next to impossible to detect it. Technically, it could only spread between computers running Windows operation systems. Even so, if an employee were to plug a USB thumb drive into an infected system, the worm would infect the thumb drive and countless other systems into which the drive was inserted.

There were many rumors doing the rounds that the attack was the handiwork of the Israel-U.S. combine. According to an article by Dan Goodin,[16] security editor at Ars Technica portal, in February 2016, it is obvious that Stuxnet comprised just one element of a much larger cyber-attack plan created by the U.S. The larger design was to take out Iran's air defenses, communications systems, as well as critical components of its power grid. Using an individual system to neutralize numerous operating systems at the Nuclear Enrichment Site in Fordow, situated deep within the mountains close to Iran's Qom city, was another element of the grand plan. An earlier piece in Ars Technica, in June 2012, by deputy editor Nate Anderson, only strengthened lingering doubts about U.S. and Israeli complicity in the incident.[17] If Nate is to be believed, the U.S. government planned out its cyberspace international strategy as early as 2011.

---

16 https://arstechnica.com/tech-policy/2016/02/massive-us-planned-cyberattack-against-iran-went-well-beyond-stuxnet/

17 https://arstechnica.com/tech-policy/2012/06/confirmed-us-israel-created-stuxnet-lost-control-of-it/

Further confirmation of the U.S.-Israeli involvement appeared in *Confront and Conceal: Obama's Secret Wars and Surprising Use of American Power Back,* a 2012 book by *New York Times* Washington correspondent David Sanger. A June 2016 report in the paper unveiled the true development and history of the Stuxnet virus. The report also mentions the worm's accidental escape from the Natanz Nuclear Facility in Iran's Isfahan Province.

In the absence of any concrete evidence, we can never be too sure about who planned the Stuxnet attack. Suffice it to say that all fingers are pointed towards the two nations. We must keep in mind that the purpose of Stuxnet was never to *"kill"* the centrifuges but to slowly degrade Iran's nuclear capabilities and prevent them from progressing anytime soon. There is speculation that the Stuxnet was configured specifically to destroy centrifuges but there is hardly any evidence to back this claim.

Jim Finkle, Reuters's cybersecurity editor, wrote in February 2013,[18] quoting cybersecurity firm Symantec's report released the same month, that Stuxnet was deployed against Iran all the way back in November 2007. The article states that Stuxnet was *"discovered"* in 2010 after the attack on Iran's uranium enrichment facility in Natanz, but it was in the system long before that. It seems Symantec's researchers had uncovered a piece of code in one of the infected machines, and they called it *"Stuxnet 0.5."* As per the Symantec report, Stuxnet 0.5 had been in development since the beginning of 2005 and deployed two years later when

---

18 https://www.reuters.com/article/us-cyberwar-stuxnet/researchers-say-stuxnet-was-deployed-against-iran-in-2007-idUSBRE91P0PP20130226

the Natanz facility went online.

According to a TED Talk video, released in March 2011,[19] featuring Ralph Langner, a German security consultant focused on control systems, the attackers behind Stuxnet feared Iran's nuclear capability. Mindful of this, they decided upon targeting the control box, so they can have the access required to manipulate the speed and behavior of the centrifuges in the nuclear processing facilities. The first challenge that the attackers encountered was that the control box was not based on a Windows system; it used an entirely different technology. Their tactic to overcome this obstacle involved planting a strong virus in one of the Windows-based systems used by the engineers to configure the control box. This virus would allow Stuxnet to spread and make its way through the control box, a simple-enough contrivance. The malware was soon deployed in the Windows computer, which loaded the Stuxnet into the controllers and then went on to target the centrifuges, thus causing the nuclear programs to fail in no time.

After working out the details of the plan, it was time to test the Stuxnet, and the attackers began to run lab tests on it. They soon realized that Stuxnet was a different kettle of fish altogether. It was not simply the complex virus they had bargained for, but slightly complicated as well. Behaviorally, it was a kind of oddball. In other words, Stuxnet is a mouse that will only go after one specific cheese; it will sniff other cheeses but will not do anything to it. For instance, if it is deployed into a program and set up to destroy a target, it would definitely work as per the command, but there was a catch. It would not harm the system if the targeted system was not running the same programs that are set in the Stuxnet to target.

The engineers along with Langner decided to lay bare the coding of the virus to understand its workings. They soon figured that it consisted of a set of programs that worked like two bombs; one big and the other small and working autonomously on separate targets. The smaller bomb went about attacking the controller box, while its bigger mate blitzed both centrifuges and the controller box. Once deployed, not even the attackers could control Stuxnet, that was the terrible beauty of it! By all accounts, the virus carried the hallmark of a professionally engineered malware, almost on the rocket science grade.

What really took Langner and his team by surprise was the pre-recorded data set in the Stuxnet virus. This was similar to what we see quite often in Hollywood flicks where a heist is taking place and a pre-recorded footage is played on the security cameras to fool the guards. Stuxnet pulled off something similar by showing a pre-recorded set of information on the screen as though everything was normal, lulling adversaries into a false sense of security, while devastating centrifuge after centrifuge in the background. This was one of the most impressive pieces of engineering Langner had encountered.

After close observation and study, the team concluded that that the attacks orchestrated by Stuxnet were of a generic nature and had nothing specific at all to do with centrifuges. The same mode of attack could be unleashed on an automobile factory or even on a power plant and the consequences would be fatal.

Ralph rounded off his disclosures about Stuxnet by pointing towards the involvement of Mossad, Israel's intelligence service, at some point in the Stuxnet attack, adding further that the U.S. was the major contributor to this lethal digital weapon.

Flame

The article by David Kushner, referenced earlier, mentioned another virus called *'Flame.'* According to this narrative, in May 2012, Kaspersky Lab was requested by the International Telecommunication Union, the United Nations agency responsible for managing information and communication technologies, to look at a different malware. It was considered a key suspect in the destruction of important data files of an oil company working out of Iran. While working on the agency's appeal, Kaspersky's automated system recognized a variant of Stuxnet.

Kaspersky's Roel Schouwenberg wasn't so easily convinced with the automated result and thought it was a system error. A thorough examination of the malware failed to reveal any of Stuxnet's obvious and common attributes. More in-depth research showed traces of another file called *"Flame."* At first, Flame and Stuxnet were thought to be independent viruses but researchers soon understood that Flame was in fact a forerunner to Stuxnet that had remained under the radar for so long.

Flame was around 20 megabytes in size and technically nearly 40 times bigger than Stuxnet; yet it had managed to evade detection. After Schouwenberg's revelation, security specialists felt Flame, like Stuxnet was the creature of a *"nation-state."* To analyze Flame more closely, Kaspersky decided to employ the sinkhole technique, which involves taking control of the virus' command-and-control server domain. The result was that when Flame attempted to establish a connection with the server within its home base, it would actually be sending information to Kaspersky's server! Despite the effort, it proved quite difficult to identify the real owner of Flame's server.

Stuxnet, on one hand, had been drawn up with a certain purpose, namely, destroy a thing while Flame was solely dedicated to spying on people. It was also dexterous enough to proliferate through, say, a USB thumb drive, or across printers plugged into the same network. So advanced was Flame's construct that once it had compromised the system, it could effortlessly access top-secret PDF files, look up keywords, and transfer a summary of that document to the server, all the while avoiding detection. Above all, Flame had the ability to transmit data with any Bluetooth-enabled device. While most viruses can only place malware in systems from a standard Bluetooth range of 30 meters, Flame could accomplish this feat over a distance of nearly two kilometers. Isn't that enough proof of its deadly impact?

The purpose of this chapter was to examine one of the earliest and biggest cyber intrusions that succeeded in physically impacting a facility in a major way. An important takeaway is the realization that hackers strike not just virtually, as is popularly imagined, but can also cause physical destruction while still hunched over their laptops, using a well-coded virus. The definition of the term *"virus"* has been evolving since the 1990s, and now encompasses far more dangerous malware that is becoming deadlier each day. The story so far is that viruses are able to physically damage facilities and steal data from afar, but as such malware becomes more and more sophisticated, they will likely test the limits of enterprises' cyber security perimeters. Every such intrusion and negative experience will only serve to shake our confidence in our cyber resilience frameworks that we once thought were impregnable. These adverse cyber events can simply make us question our own security in this connected world. Are we safe or are we not? Is our privacy being compromised? Who can tell how dangerous our data situation can become in the not-so-distant future?

Chapter Four

Sure, I Can Hold You Hostage

June 28, 2017. The President of the Smart Power Company, Paul Adams,[20] received an urgent call from Ji Viz in systems admin. The main server used for processing critical electric grid data for eastern utility companies had an issue that needed to be resolved within 24 hours. This was critical to ensure correct readings could be fed to the utility companies for their operational tasks, so they, in turn, knew how to bill customers. Without this data, utility companies would be flying blind with no record whatsoever of how much

---

20 Paul Adams is a disguised name for a person who I interviewed when his company became a target of WannaCry. While the name of the company and character are disguised; events are real and occurred in 2018.

energy a particular consumer was using. Along with affecting revenue, this also represented a great security risk and if it persisted, there was a strong possibility that customers might conclude that they couldn't trust the utility with their data. The work of Smart Power is to monitor and log operations data for public utility companies along the Eastern U.S. Their sensors are mounted every 100 feet on electrical wires and cover the entire grid. These sensors collect temperature, current, voltage, and sensitivity data, which is vitally important to the operations of utilities. Their main server showed the following screen (Figure 1) with a ransom note, which also showed up on the systems of many users affected by WannaCry ransomware.

The ransom note made no bones about the attackers' intent and purpose. The message was bold and clear; essentially, the virus had encrypted the users' files and cut off all access to these documents. The

Figure 1: Randsomware [Image sourced from: https://en.wikipedia. org/wiki/WannaCry_ransomware_attack]

ransom note demanded an upfront payment of $300 in bitcoin within the next three days, failing which the ransom money would be doubled. Victims who don't pay within seven days would have their files erased. This was business disruption of the worst order, and a small business couldn't hope to recover so quickly as to completely rebuild their system in time; nor could they be sure how much of the virus had spread to the rest of the internal systems. The local FBI office was contacted but the bigger question remained: how to regain control over business processes. Meanwhile, the hackers, for their part, would entertain only a certain number of outcomes in this situation. Eventually, the organization figured out that it was more cost effective to pay the ransom and get the business back on track, so the end result was that the organization was $300 short but up and running. "So much of hassle and loss," thought Paul, "only because an intruder had sneaked into their database and threatened to erase it." How many small companies faced with similar situations might have chosen the line of least resistance and quietly paid up 300 bitcoins?

The ransomware attack to the accompaniment of the by-now-familiar ransom notes at Smart Power Company is a textbook example of how cyber warfare works to con users and line the pockets of organized cybercriminals. Hostage taking and ransoming have come a long way, from an ancient practice, which has persisted in many parts of the world into modern times, to an online con game in which unknown scam artists hold the key assets of an individual or organization globally captive, motivated chiefly, though not always, by financial gain.

Some of the best viruses, detailed below, are used

to ransom money and get demands fulfilled, or cause massive financial and data loss for companies that reject extortion demands.

WannaCry

The heading of this chapter itself is enough to trigger the question, "How can a virus hold someone hostage?" Have a look at the worldwide cyber-attack conducted by the WannaCry ransomware cryptoworm[21] and therein lies the answer. The objective of the attack was to encrypt data on computers running the Microsoft Windows operating system. The hackers then demanded payment via bitcoin cryptocurrency. The intrusion made use of EternalBlue, an exploit developed by NSA, as admitted by several of its ex-employees, to operate and hack the Microsoft operating system.[22] This exploit was exposed by the hacker group Shadow Brokers in April 2017, a month before the WannaCry cyber-attack.

A number of things made WannaCry particularly notable. The cyber-attack affected Britain's National Health Service and exploited computers running Microsoft Windows. The ransomware reached the computer in the form of a dropper file (a self-contained program that extracts other application components embedded therein) containing resources used for encrypting data. As the program infiltrates the computer, it tries to access the hard-coded URL, the kill-switch. If, for some reason, the program cannot access a particular file, it proceeds to search for files in Microsoft Office, MKV or MP3 formats and renders them useless for the

---

21 https://www.csoonline.com/article/3227906/ransomware/what-is-wannacry-ransomware-how-does-it-infect-and-who-was-responsible.html
22 https://en.wikipedia.org/wiki/EternalBlue

user. The next logical step is to demand a ransom of $300 in bitcoin in exchange for decrypting the file.

WannaCry accessed computers by exploiting a particular aspect in Microsoft Windows' Server Message Block (SMB), a protocol that helps various nodes on a network to communicate. The protocol could be tricked by sending in specially crafted packages of arbitrary codes. It is believed that NSA came across this vulnerability, but instead of reporting it to Microsoft, they made an exploit called EternalBlue, which, in turn, was stolen by Shadow Brokers and leaked to an online dump in April 2017. The exploit was spotted by Microsoft released a patch though many machines were still affected. When it became known that NSA had actually been aware of the vulnerability sooner but had chosen not to share the information, they were discredited by Microsoft.

There was a supposed kill-switch built in to the WannaCry program, just in case the developers of the ransomware wanted to pull the plug, and this was discovered by Marcus Hutchins, a British security researcher. He noticed WannaCry trying to contact the hard-coded URL and if it could access the code, then it would shut itself down.

Estonia DDOS

A cyber-attack[23] was allegedly launched by Russia in April 2007, on Estonia, and mainly targeted the following web sites:

• The Estonian Presidency and its Parliament

---

23 https://www.theguardian.com/world/2007/may/17/topstories3.russia

- Almost all of the Government Ministries
- Political parties
- Three of the country's six biggest news organizations
- Two banks
- Firms specializing in communication

These distributed denial of service (DDOS) attacks are believed to have been in response to the relocation by Estonians of a Second World War memorial on April 27, 2007, which drew protests, organized by ethnic Russians.[24] DDOS occurs when a website is visited by tens of thousands of people, results in overcrowding of the servers' bandwidth, thus shutting down the website completely. Security officials who traced the internet address, say the initial attacks were carried out by Russians.

In response, Estonians were quick to limit the access of foreign entities to their websites, which meant only domestic users in Estonia could access the sites. A fallout of this precautionary measure was that Estonia was cut off from the rest of the world. The attack was reportedly so severe that the country's defense ministry spokesperson Mikko Maddis said they were lucky to have just survived the attack. The hack was so serious that it was termed *"WebWar One."* This was also the first instance of an entire nation being targeted on almost every digital front, all at once.

The attacks happened over a period of 21 days, starting April 27, 2007, when ethnic Russians clashed

---

24 https://www.computerworld.com/article/2541477/security0/expert--russian-government-ruled-out-in-estonia-ddos-attacks.html

with Estonian police, and then reached peaks on May 3, and then on May 8 and 9. This is considered the first instance of a DDOS on such a mega scale. In January 2008, a 19-year-old was arrested in Tallinn, Estonia, for his role in the attack.

Initially, Russia was blamed for the attacks though Russian officials denied they had anything to do with it. Because there was a lot of problem tracing back the source of the attack from Tallinn all the way to Moscow, it was possible to cast doubts about Russia's accountability (plausible deniability) for the attack. Even a direct line could not be connected from Moscow to Tallinn.

Ashley Madison

Ashley Madison started in 2001 as a dating website which facilitated discreet dating for adults. An attack began on their servers on July 12, 2015.[25] When Ashley Madison employees logged on to their computers; they found a message that threatened to leak client information unless both Ashley Madison and its companion site (Established Men) stopped operating. The hacker group, *The Impact Team*, released information on two of Ashley Madison's clients on July 15, 2015, to prove their legitimacy.

On July 20, Avid Life Media, the cheating website's parent company launched an internal investigation, contacted the police, and hired Cycura, a cybersecurity firm. It also acknowledged the hack in a press release.

When Ashley Madison failed to comply with the

---

25 https://www.thestar.com/business/2015/08/24/
police-timeline-of-the-ashley-madison-hack.html

demands of *The Impact Team*, data of more than 30 million users was released on August 17, 2015. two days later, emails of Avid Life Media CEO Noel Biderman, along with source codes and internal data, was exposed, accompanied by a taunting message: "Hey Noel, you can admit... it's real now."

On August 21, 2015, in an interview with Vice digital media, *The Impact Team* claimed to be in possession of 300 gigabytes of data, adding that it was easy to infiltrate the Ashley Madison website. On August 23, the hackers leaked a third dump of data, and this release was particularly damaging since it contained info on government personnel.

On August 24, 2015, Ashley Madison was hit with a $578 million class action lawsuit brought by two firms on behalf of all Canadians. The same day, Ashley Madison offered a reward of $500,000 for any information linked to the hackers. Author Brian Krebs of KrebsOnSecurity.com fame wrote an article that implied the founding CTO of Ashley Madison, Raja Bhatia, had hacked the website Nerve.com, a competitor. The leaked email dump also included messages from Mark Steele, Ashley Madison's director of security, that warned Biderman of vulnerabilities in the website, such as multiple cross-site scripting and cross-site request forgeries.

On August 25-26, 2015, there were more data leaks and eventually extortion attempts by hackers on users whose data had been exposed. There were many instances of public shaming of victims, divorce proceedings by spouses of users outed by the hack, and even a few suicides. On August 28, 2015, CEO Biderman stepped down.

On September 9, 2015, a security researcher, Gabor Szathmari, claimed to have discovered poor security measures taken by Ashley Madison to secure their users' information. The site did not use email or phone validation to prevent bots signing up. Gabor's disclosure also shed light on ways in which the attack might have been orchestrated.

On September 10, a blog post revealed that Ashley Madison did not have effective measures in place to encrypt and secure sensitive data while its customers did not care to use strong passwords and, oddly enough, *"123456"* was the most common password! This might have helped the hackers crack 11 million passwords in a matter of 10 days.

In addition to all of the security issues that Ashley Madison ignored, there was also the not-so-small matter of there being almost no women registered[26] on the site. Men paid the cheating site substantial amounts to get credits, so they would be able to message a real girl but were reportedly shortchanged, without realizing it of course, and ended up messaging bots. It is arguable that the adultery site never promised easy hook-ups; even so, this looked like a clever marketing trick designed to nudge hopeful male users into paying more and more to meet women, when they were actually talking to automated bots. Following this strategy, Ashley Madison raked in $115.5 million in revenue in 2014 alone.

In all of the previous examples, we see the recurring trend of one entity holding another hostage by infiltrating their website and collecting sensitive data.

26 https://gizmodo.com/the-fembots-of-ashley-madison-1726670394

In the case of WannaCry, the objective was to encrypt a user's important files and then pocket a ransom in exchange for decrypting the file. The object held hostage is the file. In the Estonian DDOS incident, websites of the government ministries and news networks experienced an overload of users. At one level, the attack was a retaliatory measure for relocating a Soviet-era war memorial; however, in the process, Estonian websites and their users were held hostage to bring pressure on Estonia's authorities to restore the memorial to its original location. Lastly, in the Ashley Madison data leak, the demand was simple: take down two of the websites since they were in the *"morally repugnant"* business of helping married people have affairs, at least from the hackers' standpoint. One of the sites matched well-established men with young women to be their *"sugar daddies"* and this was also demanded to be taken down.[27]

As one sees in the flow of the book, the objective of hacking has changed substantially and has evolved to become nefarious and dark.

---

27 https://www.youtube.com/watch?v=U_pzHXfn8dE

Case Study Two

Cheating Website Gets Cheated On: Ashley Madison Data Breach

The Ashley Madison Agency, or simply Ashley Madison, is a Toronto, Canada, based online dating service for married people seeking extramarital affairs, described variously by the media as an *"adultery-enabling website," "infidelity dating site," "married dating site," "cheating site,"* and *"affair-focused dating site."* Users can sign up for a free account using an email address, which Ashley Madison didn't verify, or users were not required to validate, so fake or borrowed email addresses could be used. For instance, a user could create an account on this website with the address *donald.trump@whitehouse.gov* without Mr. Trump's knowledge. While the basic account was free, users were charged extra for premium features like chatting. The site's *"Delete Everything"* was one such paid option that charged users $19 to get their personal data on the site completely *"scrubbed"* (erased) without a trace.

In July 2015, Ashley Madison, with its signature tagline, "Life is short. Have an affair," boasted 37 million members across 53 countries but predominantly in Canada and the U.S. From 2009 to 2014, Ashley Madison's revenues grew four-fold, touching 115 million, driven by a solid growth in female users, according to the company's CEO. The revenue was projected to exceed $150 million in 2015 on the back of a membership surge in culturally conservative markets around the world. Ashley Madison was the biggest website in its parent company, Avid Life Media's (ALM's) portfolio, which includes other match-making portals like Cougar Life, which promises to connect older women with younger men; Established Men, which aspires to bring together beautiful young women and rich sugar daddies to *"fulfill their lifestyle needs;"* and The Big and the Beautiful, for overweight dating.

How It Started

Darren Morgenstern of Toronto, Canada, resident, opened a brick and mortar dating service in early 2002, where people walked in, paid a fee, and registered their profile. Morgenstern named the agency *"Ashley Madison,"* joining two of the most popular female names in North America; besides Madison was a pretty nice-sounding name that obscured the underlying business of enabling adultery. As the Internet expanded rapidly in the early 2000s, he put his entire business online. Business stabilized, and Morgenstern sold Ashley Madison to ALM in 2007. Ashley Madison expanded into new markets under Noel Biderman, a former lawyer and sports agent who took over as CEO of Ashley Madison and ALM in 2007.

Noel Biderman

Biderman is a Canadian, multimillionaire, father of two, who claimed to be happily married and says that he would be devastated if his wife cheated on him. He has consistently maintained that he was not in the business of promoting infidelity but providing a safe place for affairs to take place if; in the nature of things, they are going to happen. Ashley Madison was intended to be a place where people can be honest with each other. Biderman claims that one reason he created the site is that thirty percent of the people on single websites are not single at all. He revealed in 2010 that he made "tons of millions" from Ashley Madison but stopped short of mentioning the exact figure. Biderman was pictured on the website with a wide beaming smile and a single, shushing finger placed in front of his lips. He has been filleted, to no end, on popular shows such as The Larry King Show, Ellen, and Dr Phil.

The Hack

On July 15, 2015, an individual or more likely a group, calling itself *The Impact Team*' claimed to have hacked into Ashley Madison's user databases, financial account information, and various other proprietary data. Perhaps to show they were serious, the group posted scraps of data they had pilfered from nearly 40 million users from across Ashley Madison and its companion sites. The group also exposed maps of the company's internal servers, details of its bank account, salary information, as well as data from the network accounts used by employees.

In a statement, the hackers threatened to release customers' personal information in 30 days if ALM didn't permanently shut down its biggest hookup dating site, Ashley Madison, and its companion site, Established Men: *"ALM has been instructed to take Ashley Madison and Established Men offline permanently in all forms, or we will release all customer records, including profiles with all the customers' secret sexual fantasies and matching credit card transactions, real names and addresses, and employee documents and emails."*

The Impact Team spared Cougar Life, another ALM dating site, but seemed bent on taking Ashley Madison and Established Men to task, not simply for their laissez-faire attitude to infidelity, but also for unfair business practices. In a long manifesto posted alongside the stolen data, the hackers said they decided to expose this data to nail alleged lies Ashley Madison had told its customers about the site's *"Delete Everything"* feature that cost customers $19 to enable. With the *"Delete Everything"* or *"Full Delete"* option, customers enjoyed the privilege (or so they thought) of getting the website scrubbed of all their personally identifiable information (PII) such as their real name, address, site usage history, purchase details, and credit card data.

On July 21, 2015, the hackers exposed the intensely personal details of two subscribers: one man in Canada and the other in Brockton, Massachusetts. On August 18, 2015, the cyberwarriors struck again with a vengeance, this time offloading 9.7 gigabyte of data on to the dark web accessible only via the Tor anonymizing browser. The file contained names, logins, passwords, addresses, and phone numbers for as many as 32 million Ashley Madison users. Arguably, many users would have registered using random numbers and addresses, besides borrowed emails. Still, the leaked database also included transaction data going back to 2008 for millions of payments. There was a four-digit number corresponding to each such payment transaction and this could be the last four digits of the user's credit card number or a unique transaction ID. Real names and addresses of members could be harvested from these digits except where users had made payments via anonymous pre-paid cards that do not leave any payment trail.

Passwords in leaked data were hashed using bcrypt, considered a more secure hashing algorithm than MD5, but determined hackers might still manage to crack into the hash and scoop out the subscriber's original password, using which, they could exfiltrate the person's private messages available online.

The descriptive messages in the data dump confirmed what was already known about male sexual fantasies. One member whose account mapped to the name and phone number of an employee with Canada's Customs and Immigration Union as well as an Ottawa address wrote: *"I like lots of foreplay and stamina, fun, discretion, oral, even willingness to experiment – *smile*."*

The worst was still to come, and this time it was going to be up close and personal for none other than Biderman himself. On August 20, 2015, a 30-gigabyte data dump, containing, among other things, nearly 200,000 emails belonging to Noel Biderman, surfaced online. BuzzFeed digital media reported that the leaked emails suggested the Ashley Madison founder had multiple affairs, including one with a student badly in need of some money, and another with an escort. A little more than a year earlier, chatting up with Daily News, the chirpy entrepreneur had sounded much like a self-proclaimed champion of family values, claiming he has not had an affair yet. Biderman was quoted as saying, "If I wanted to have an affair, I would have one... My wife is 39, so I'm walking on eggshells."[28]

Talking to the BBC in August 2015, Per Thorsheim, a leading security consultant with a singular focus on passwords, confirmed the emails were genuine and that that the email had to come from the CEO's mailbox. Ashley Madison's Response:

On July 19, 2015, Ashley Madison Chief Executive Noel Biderman confirmed the hack and said the website was working *"diligently and feverishly"* to mitigate the risks involved. He hinted that the alleged hack might be the work of a one-time insider, like a former employee or contractor who enjoyed access to the company's networks and was probably hands-on with its technical services. Talking to KrebsonSecurity, Biderman seemed confident that they were very close to unmasking the culprit: *"We're not denying this happened...Like us or not, this is still a criminal act... We're on the doorstep of [confirming] who we believe is the culprit... I've got their profile right in front of me, all their work credentials."*[29]

ALM soon realized it was time to get its act together

28 Joseph Bernstein; "Leaked Emails Suggest Ashley Madison Founder Had Multiple Affairs;" BuzzFeed News; August 26, 2015; https://www.buzzfeednews.com/article/josephbernstein/leaked-emails-suggest-ashley-madison-founder-had-multiple-af

29 KrebsOnSecurity; "Online Cheating Site AshleyMadison Hacked;" July 15, 2015; https://krebsonsecurity.com/2015/07/online-cheating-site-ashleymadison-hacked/

to win back customer confidence, badly and inevitably shaken up by the alleged data breach. Toronto-based cybersecurity firm Cycura and Joel Eriksson, its CTO, were soon engaged to judge the nature of the hack and the extent of damage caused. ALM maintained a studied silence in the days following the initial hack, though it released a statement about the attack on its website and Twitter (@ashleymadison):

"We have always had the confidentiality of our customers' information foremost in our minds, and have had stringent security measures in place... As other companies have experienced, these security measures have unfortunately not prevented this attack to our system... We are working with law enforcement agencies, which are investigating this criminal act... Any and all parties responsible for this act of cyber-terrorism will be held responsible."

After the August 2015 leak, Ashley Madison said: "This event is not an act of hacktivism; it is an act of criminality. It is an illegal action against the individual members of AshleyMadison.com, as well as any freethinking people who choose to engage in fully lawful online activities... We will not sit idly by and allow these thieves to force their personal ideology on citizens around the world."

Two months prior to the Ashley Madison incident, it was reported that the 64-million-member AdultFriendFinder, another dating site, had been hacked by Hell, a dark web hacking forum. In a brief titled, *"Risky Business for AshleyMadison.com,"* Wall Street Journal observed: *"Given the breach at*

AdultFriendFinder, investors will have to think of hack attacks as a risk factor... And given its business' reliance on confidentiality, prospective AshleyMadison investors should hope it has sufficiently, girded its loins."[30] Some of the exposed documents suggest that internally Ashley Madison had nagging concerns about the security of its business data. A Microsoft Excel sheet showed that the leadership had sought responses from employees on what they thought were the key risks facing the company. In retrospect, Trevor Stokes, Ashley Madison's chief technology officer's answer was spot-on: *"Security... I would hate to see our systems hacked and/or the leak of personal information."*[31]

Hackers' Motivation

The Ashley Madison hack was of a different genre than routine intrusions for ill-gotten gain. Speaking on *"CBS This Morning"* in July 2015, business analyst Jill Schlesinger remarked: *"I think the motivation for the hackers is to embarrass the company."* Highly motivated hackers can be determined to get into sites like this, looking for intimate or embarrassing details, says Dr. Michael Sulmeyer of the Belfer Center's Cyber Project Director at the Harvard Kennedy School.

Human Cost

Just a week after the breach, its devastating repercussions were being felt. By August 25, 2015, social news aggregator sites, like Reddit, were bursting

---

30 Miriam Gottfried; "Risky Business for Ashley Madison.com;" May 22, 2015; https://blogs.wsj.com/moneybeat/2015/05/22/risky-business-for-ashleymadison-com/
31 KrebsOnSecurity; "Online Cheating Site AshleyMadison Hacked;" July 15, 2015; https://krebsonsecurity.com/2015/07/online-cheating-site-ashleymadison-hacked/#more-31650

left, right and center with stories of cheated spouses confronting partners, throwing in their face the evidence they had come by online. The paparazzi media machine was fine-combing the data for names of celebrities, political leaders, and religious higher-ups. Multiple websites like CheckAshleyMadison.com popped up in no time after the hack to help people figure out if their email or phone number was in the leaked database or not. Ashley Madison members often received emails from unnamed extortionists threatening to humiliate the recipients by contacting their family unless they paid up, anonymously using bitcoin.

Gawker blog site reported, based on data from the hack, that a credit card in the name of Josh Duggar, star of reality show *"19 Kids and Counting"* aired on TLC television channel, had been used to pay for at least one of two memberships of Ashley Madison. At the time when the first account was created, Duggar was married to wife Anna for at least five years. Duggar was executive director of FRC Action, which champions traditional family values. Data associated with Duggar's Ashley Madison account suggested that he was looking for a partner for a series of sexual activities ranging from conventional to oral sex, to *"dabbling in roles involving sexual toys."* On August 24, 2015, John Gibson, a pastor and seminary professor with a sense of humor, married with two children, committed suicide after he was outed by the hack.

Scottish lawmaker Michelle Thomson said hackers had harvested his obsolete email address and used it to register an account with the site. Likewise, Talab Abu Arar, a Bedouin Arab parliamentarian in Israel, told Israel's Army Radio: *"Someone wanted simply to hurt my good name ... it is very annoying."*

Another disturbing discovery by a researcher with the Twitter handle t0x0pg, was that there was more than 15,000 U.S. military and government email addresses (e.g., State Department, Department of Homeland Security) among the leaked pile of data. Some of these might have been fake, but chances are that several others might have been real, which meant PII of several thousand military personnel – a majority of them male, since only one out of every ten Ashley Madison users was reportedly female - was in the public domain for anyone to gawk at.

Moreover, when an account was created using the Ashley Madison app, and even if the subscriber used a fake email address, the app would report his/her real GPS coordinates (latitude, longitude). This along with addresses, phone numbers, and passwords might be of interest to organized crime syndicates, social media disinformation campaigners often backed by America's adversaries, and foreign intelligence services. As a consequence, any military personnel who signed up for an account with Ashley Madison would be in violation of the U.S. Department of Defense policy which prohibits the use of military computers or email addresses to view pornography or sign up with a porn or dating site. Any person violating this policy could be punished with a dishonorable discharge, in which case, they would stand to forfeit all military benefits.

Paris-based CybelAngel mapped 1,230 of the adultery site's users to Saudi Arabia based on their ".sa" domain extension though, some of these could also have been used by expats outside the country. In any case, these are official email addresses not personal ones. The country's Shari'ah (Islamic) law allows the death penalty for *"serious criminal offences"* like adultery and homosexuality.

Ashley Madison: Post the Hack

The data breach came at a time when the adultery site was looking to debut its $200 million IPO on the London Stock Exchange. In April 2015, Biderman seemed firmly determined to go ahead with the listing, and for almost two months, the company organized financial roadshows to appeal to potential investors. However, by July 2015, he seemed to be backtracking on the IPO, citing endless reasons. He told Business Insider in July 2015 that the buzz around the potential IPO and the awareness it created had expanded the options before the company, adding that stock exchange listing was no longer its No. 1 choice. Biderman was in no mood to concede that the data hack had ruined his proposed IPO party, at least for the moment, since investors often consider a company's cyber security plans and risks to its operations from third-parties: *"We are not a typical tech company and we have a subscriptions model. We never wanted to launch an IPO because we had to, or to get funding to keep the lights on, we just thought it was one of the best options for expanding and giving good returns to shareholders."[32]*

On August 23, 2015, BBC reported that Ashley Madison's parent company was facing a $576 million class-action lawsuit brought by two Canadian firms, Charney Lawyers and Sutts as well as Strosberg LLP, on behalf of *"all Canadians"* hit by the data breach. On August 28, 2015, Noel Biderman stepped down as CEO of ALM Inc. Ever since, it appears that Biderman has been in the business of distancing his online persona from Ashley Madison and ALM. His four websites and revamped Twitter account serve up the rebooted image

---

32   Lianna Brinded; "Ashley Madison is close to abandoning its London IPO;" Business Insider – Money & Markets; July 4, 2015

of a nicer Noel, smiling a little wider, a quintessential Canadian and responsible citizen who divides his time between respectable business consulting and philanthropic community work. However, the names Ashley Madison and ALM are nowhere to be seen.

In July 2016, ALM, parent company of the by-now infamous Ashley Madison, re-branded itself to a new avatar - Ruby Corp. The libertine tagline *"Life is Short. Have an Affair"* was trashed within a month and a new one *"Find Your Moment"* announced. The imagery of a woman wearing a wedding ring on the brand's login page gave way to a red gem-shaped logo. In December 2016, Ruby agreed to pay $1.66 million, though without accepting liability, to settle a probe by the U.S. Federal Trade Commission and several states into serious data security lapses and fraudulent practices. On July 14, 2017, the adultery website agreed to pay $11.2 million to settle a U.S. class action suit brought on behalf of nearly 37 million users whose personal details were exposed by the data scam while continuing to deny any wrongdoing. This works out to up to $3,500 in compensation for Ashley Madison users, provided they are able to back their claims with valid documentation.

Chapter Five

John Podesta's Time in the Barrel Will Come

The 2016 U.S. presidential elections were riddled with often questionable strategies used on behalf of the two main contenders: Donald Trump and Hillary Clinton. Both camps employed numerous tactics in order to defame their opponent and convince of their own ideas. Of course, their campaign strategies were vastly different, but the common denominator with both candidates was that they had a lot of explaining to do with respect to their past ventures, comments on key issues, and proximity to important foreign dignitaries.

The presidential hopefuls hit a new level when they resorted to cyber warfare to gain the upper hand in a hard-fought campaign. During the entire race for the White House, Trump and Clinton were going neck and neck, but Clinton was always ahead. Then the unexpected happened. In early October 2016, The Washington Post published a video in which Trump was heard having an extremely lewd conversation with Access Hollywood show's co-host Billy Bush about TV host and entertainment journalist Nancy O'Dell. Billy Bush is also heard passing comments on women. Time magazine stated in their article: *"The bombshell dropped on The Washington Post's website just after 4 pm: a video of Donald Trump, in 2005, using extremely vulgar language to describe women, detailing his attempt to bed a married woman and bragging that he can grope women because he is a celebrity."*[33]

Trump was recorded saying: *"I moved on her, and I failed. I'll admit it. I did try and f**k her. She was married,"* says Trump, while the video lingers on the exterior of the bus.

"And I moved on her very heavily. In fact, I took her out furniture shopping. She wanted to get some furniture. I said, 'I'll show you where they have some nice furniture.' I moved on her like a bitch, but I couldn't get there. And she was married. Then all of a sudden, I see her, she's now got the big phony tits and everything. She's totally changed her look."

---

33 http://www.politifact.com/truth-o-meter/ statements/2016/dec/18/john-podesta/its-true-wikileaks-dumped-podesta-emails-hour-afte/

After this, both of them appear to notice actress Arianne Zucker, star of the soap opera *Days of Our Lives,* who acted alongside Trump for the cameo. Zucker is waiting to escort them into the TV studio.

"Whoa!" Trump is heard telling Bush when he sees Zucker. *"I've got to use some Tic Tacs, just in case I start kissing her. You know I'm automatically attracted to beautiful – I just start kissing them. It's like a magnet. Just kiss. I don't even wait. And when you're a star, they let you do it. You can do anything."*

"You can do anything," Trump says, as heard in the video, *"Grab them by the pu**y."*

After they get off the bus and meet Zucker, Bush tells Zucker, *"How about a little hug for the Donald? He just got off the bus."* Trump then hugs Zucker and says, *"Melania said this was okay."*

The media was quick to capitalize on that video as Trump and Bush had openly degraded women as a whole. The Trump campaign promptly issued a statement and an apology for the sexually derogatory remarks after the video leak, with the Republican candidate apologizing sheepishly *"if anyone was offended..."* by his remarks.[34]

It was alleged by the New York Post that Billy Bush bragged sometime in August 2016 about having a video of Trump that showed *"Trump being a real dog,"*

---

34 https://www.rollingstone.com/politics/news/trump-makes-vulgar-comments-about-women-in-leaked-2005-video-w444000

which was overheard by some NBC reporters, and that was how this whole scandal unfolded.[35] On October 3, 2016, NBC claimed to have heard the tape and began working on different stories. The following day, the video was forwarded to NBC's legal department, where it remained for 2-3 days.

On October 7, 2016, NBC News was still waiting for some internal processes to be completed as well as gathering some comments on the video, including from the Trump camp. However, this got delayed since Hurricane Matthew was the big story of the day. So, Access Hollywood's producers decided to push their story on the tape to Monday, after the second presidential debate. NBC News agreed to let Access Hollywood go out with the tape first, since it came from the show.

On the same day, at about 11 pm, a person, thought to be part of NBC, got frustrated with the delay and leaked the video to *The Washington Post's* David Fahrenthold, who then asked NBC about the tape.[36]

Meanwhile, the Clinton campaign had little to gloat about. In less than an hour, whistleblowing site WikiLeaks published more than 2,000 emails from what was, allegedly, the personal account of the chair

---

35 http://www.businessinsider.com/how-the-donald-trump-tape-got-leaked-2016-10#august-2016-the-new-york-post-reported-that-billy-bush-while-covering-the-rio-olympics-bragged-about-having-a-tape-of-trump-being-a-real-dog-nbc-staffers-overheard-and-thats-reportedly-how-the-search-for-the-tape-started-1
36 Ibid

of Clinton's presidential campaign, John Podesta.[37] The timing of the release and the coincidence were too hard to miss. Podesta did take notice of this and tweeted: *"On October 7, the Access Hollywood tape comes out. One hour later, WikiLeaks starts dropping my emails."*[38] The trove of emails included references to Clinton's lucrative paid speeches to banks and provided evidence of her pro-Wall Street sympathies, which seemed to run contrary to her public posturing. The timing of WikiLeaks' revelation was very convenient, and many believed this was done in an effort to tip the scales in Trump's favor.

Podesta later pointed out (and so did Shawn Henry, president of the cybersecurity firm that probed the DNC hacks, and Marc Elias, an attorney who served as general counsel on the Clinton campaign) that FBI and WikiLeaks damaged the campaign. He reportedly said:

> *"I think to this day it's inexplicable that they [FBI] were so casual about the investigation of the Russian penetration of the DNC emails. They didn't even bother to send an agent to the DNC; they left a couple of messages at the IT help desk saying, 'You might want to be careful. There are at least forces within the FBI that wanted her to lose.'"*[39]

The timing of the chain of events – coming an hour after the release of the Access Hollywood tape – raised

---

37 http://www.politifact.com/truth-o-meter/
statements/2016/dec/18/john-podesta/its-true-wikileaks-
dumped-podesta-emails-hour-afte/
38 Ibid
39 Igor Bobic; "John Podesta says 'Forces Within The FBI'
Wanted Hillary Clinton To Lose;" HuffPost; 02/12/2017

many eyebrows and was just too convenient to let slide without an investigation. Later in May 2017, Robert Mueller was appointed special counsel to investigate Russian interference with the presidential election, and Podesta was among those interviewed by Mueller's team. *The Washington Post* released the Access Hollywood video on October 7, 4:03 pm and WikiLeaks' Podesta emails came at 4:32 pm. Though they had access to this information for the past six months, WikiLeaks chose that very moment to reveal it. In all likelihood, to move the conversation away from Access Hollywood. The Trump campaign possibility had backchannel communications with WikiLeaks and advance knowledge about the Podesta hacking. In March 2019, Mueller's team indicted 34 persons, including some of Trump's top advisors and 12 Russian nationals, though the two-year-long investigation didn't uncover any evidence that the Trump campaign conspired with the Russians to influence the presidential election.

On August 21, 2016, Roger Stone, Trump's long-time confidante, tweeted: *"Trust me, it will soon [be] Podesta's time in the barrel. #CrookedHillary."* Podesta didn't know that he was hacked until October 7, 2016. Stone also claimed to have communicated with WikiLeaks and Guccifer 2.0, persona of a mysterious Russian-linked hacker believed to have leaked the DNC emails to WikiLeaks. Stone took the claim back, but this was no use as *The Atlantic* magazine had already published a partial transcript of his chats with WikiLeaks.

The head of Cambridge Analytica, a political consultancy that ran Trump's digital operations, reached out to WikiLeaks founder Julian Assange during the presidential campaign with an offer to help collate the hacked emails. Trump Jr. and WikiLeaks also exchanged direct messages on Twitter throughout the last month of the campaign and well into Trump's transition into Presidency.[40]

WikiLeaks

The mastermind behind WikiLeaks was Julian Assange, an Australian computer programmer and activist, who founded the whistleblower site in 2006. Previously, in 1991, he had pleaded guilty to cybercrime in Australia but due to his age, he was only given minimal punishment. The inspiration behind WikiLeaks was Daniel Ellsberg's 1971 release of Pentagon Papers, a top-secret study of the role the US played in Indochina from World War II until May 1968. Ellsberg turned over these documents to the *New York Times*.[41] The time lapse between Ellsberg giving the documents to New York Times and them being published was almost two years. To streamline and shrink this process, Assange created WikiLeaks.

In 2006 he wrote a series of Essays, which are now being closely studied and reveal his disgust for authoritarian, conspiracy-ridden, and highly secretive governments.[42] The same year, he created the design for WikiLeaks in Australia but soon shifted his operations to servers in Sweden, known for its press-protection laws. After all, WikiLeaks was basically created as a whistle-blowing site and they needed a platform to build upon, where they would be secure against governments

---

40 https://themoscowproject.org/dispatch/trump-wikileaks-timeline/

41 https://www.britannica.com/topic/Pentagon-Papers

42 https://www.technologyreview.com/s/421949/everything-you-need-to-know-about-wikileaks/

or entities which sought to harm them for revealing the skeletons in their closets.

WikiLeaks' website says:

> *"WikiLeaks will accept restricted or censored material of political, ethical, diplomatic or historical significance. We do not accept rumor, opinion, other kinds of firsthand accounts or material that is publicly available elsewhere."*

WikiLeaks made headlines in April 2010 with *"Collateral Murder,"* a top-secret video footage of a Reuters journalist, his driver, and several civilians being gunned down from a U.S. military helicopter in Eastern Baghdad in 2007. In July 2010, the site exposed Afghan War logs, followed by Iraq War logs in October 2010. At the end of November 2010, WikiLeaks put out a series of about 250,000 diplomatic cables acquired from an anonymous source. The combined trove of documents, numbering nearly 700,000, came from a single source: U.S. Army intelligence analyst (private first class) Bradley Manning who served in Iraq between October 2009 and May 2010.[43]

All the access that WikiLeaks has into people's private information is not just a result of hacking into the people's lives. There are also other ways to gain information more easily through the dark web, part of the internet that lies concealed beneath search engines and is typically accessed using The Onion Router (TOR), an open-source browser that supports anonymous communication.

---

43 https://www.technologyreview.com/s/421949/ everything-you-need-to-know-about-wikileaks/

WikiLeaks has used the dark web several times, so whistleblowers can chat with them about their leaks as well as to gain access to personal information. Bradley Manning first chatted up with WikiLeaks using Jabber instant messaging service and IRC before using TOR to leak her cache of documents from the U.S. military and diplomats, now billed as the largest leak of classified information in U.S. history.

WikiLeaks has been using TOR since its very start. Even back then, the site was using volunteers, and one of them mined over a million documents in December 2006 about a Somali rebel leader who was encouraging the use of hired gunmen to assassinate government officials. That was the first major leak.[44] WikiLeaks even created a page to instruct the user on how to manually configure Firefox browser to be able to use TOR. The site also lists a broken hidden service link that was once used as its anonymous dead drop (dead letter box) for uploading documents.[45]

TOR works by routing a web page request through a plethora of proxy servers in at least three random cities before finally connecting to the requested website. For instance, if someone accesses a website in, say, Houston, then the request is routed through Beijing, then Tokyo, before the person is able to login to the desired website. This in turn leaves the IP address of the computing device used by the person unidentifiable and completely anonymous. However, since the data has to move through a lot of servers to ensure it is indeed untraceable, the exercise can be quite time

---

44 https://www.britannica.com/topic/WikiLeaks
45 https://www.deepdotweb.com/2015/05/06/planning-a-leak-chat-with-wikileaks-via-a-new-tor-hidden-service/

consuming.[46,47] TOR has thousands of volunteers all over the planet and more than 7,000 routes/relays to choose from.

The dark web was first implemented by U.S. Navy researchers to allow intelligence agents to use the internet without being traced.[48] According to Ranker digital media, the information on the dark web is very vast and includes:[49]

- Credit Card Numbers - on the dark web, you can find credit card numbers in hundreds at incredibly cheap prices.

- Fake Passports - website on the dark web called *"Fake Document Services"* sells passports from every nation, including the U.S., for about $1000.

- Stolen Social Security Numbers - A site called *"Black Bank"* offers *"fresh social security numbers with credit scores above 750."*

- Hacked Government Data

Days after the U.S. Government's Office of Personnel Management was infiltrated, confidential data was stolen; traces of this stolen ware have started creeping up on the dark web.

---

46 https://www.csoonline.com/article/3249765/data-breach/what-is-the-dark-web-why-and-how-to-visit-this-invisible-part-of-the-internet.html

47 https://www.cnbc.com/2018/04/13/the-dark-web-and-how-to-access-it.html

48 https://www.wikileaks.org/wiki/WikiLeaks:Tor?

49 https://www.ranker.com/list/things-you-can-buy-on-the-dark-web/mike-rothschild

The anonymity that the dark web affords users makes it a preferred destination for selling information that would otherwise be hard to sell, undetected. Basically, anyone can use the dark web to do anything and hope to get away with it!

Case Study Three

WikiLeaks Founder Julian Assange: A Portrait in Grayscale

Come what may, the *"genius provocateur"* wouldn't reveal his age, saying only that he was born in the 1970s simply because he preferred to *"keep the bastards guessing."* Public domain data reveal however that WikiLeaks founder and computer programmer Julian Assange was born July 3, 1971 in Townsville on the north-eastern coast of Queensland, Australia, to tough-minded, non-conformist parents. His mother, Christine Ann Hawkins, daughter of Warren Hawkins, a hidebound traditional Australian academician, had abruptly decided to ride out of her hometown to Sidney – 1,500 miles away – at 17 on a motorbike bought with money she got by selling her paintings. While in Sidney, she soon melted into the city's counterculture.

Two years later, in 1970, at a Vietnam War demonstration in Sidney, Christine met John Shipton, then 26, anti-war activist, freelance builder by profession, WikiLeaks Party secretary since 2015, and most importantly, Julian's biological dad, from whom he inherited the *"rebel gene."* Shipton's relationship with Christine ended on a friendly note when she was in her early 20s and eight weeks pregnant with Julian. Bizarre as it might seem, Julian never got around to see his natural father till sometime in the mid-'90s at a meeting arranged by Christine. Julian stumbled on similarities in their mental make-up; both dad and son were drawn to the writings of Dostoevsky, Kafka, and Arthur Koestler.

Following her split with Shipton, Christine moved to Lismore in New South Wales state, where she would meet Brett Assange, who is credited with raising Julian from age 1, and giving Julian his surname. Through the rest of the '70s and '80s, Christine and Brett ran a small puppet theater. Years later, Brett Assange would remember Julian as a *"very bright boy with a keen sense of right and wrong... a sharp kid who always fought for the underdog... He had a really good sense of equality and equity."*[50]

When Julian was eight, Christine, besotted with Leif Meynell, left Brett. Leif was some kind of an amateur musician. Blonde-haired and good looking, Leif belonged to *"The Family,"* an Australian doomsday

50 CNN Wire Staff; "The secret life of Julian Assange;" Indianapolis Recorder Newspaper; Nov. 3, 2011; http://www.indianapolisrecorder.com/news/international/article_ab207d6a-0640-11e1-903f-001cc4c002e0.html

cult founded in the mid-'60s. In 1982, at the end of a tempestuous and abusive relationship, Christine fled with both sons - Julian and the son she had with Leif in 1980. Christine felt threatened that Leif might take away Julian's half-brother from her. Now hysterical and on the run from her psychopathic ex-husband, for the next five years, Christine changed houses, towns, and even her name. By the time, Julian turned 14, the terrified mother and kids who had run afoul of a maniac had moved nearly 37 times.

Both Julian and his half-brother didn't receive any formal education because their mom believed classroom learning sowed in pupils an unhealthy respect for authority. For the most part, Julian took recourse to self-education, spending time in libraries and attending correspondence classes.

Julian's early impressionable years were filled with outdoor adventure like building rafts, going fishing, descending into mine shafts and emerging after a while, and crawling in and out of tunnels. Most of his childhood *"was pretty Tom Sawyer."* School friends say Julian's family was very alternative, adding, it was *"quite exciting to go to their house."*

His early years in Queensland seems to have left a deep impression on Julian: *"I grew up in a Queensland country town where people spoke their minds bluntly... WikiLeaks was created around these core values."* In the late '80s, when he was 16/17, Julian, his mother, and brother found themselves occupying a ramshackle home at the foot of Melbourne's Dandenong Ranges. Around this time, he met an *"intelligent but introverted 16-year-old"* local girl Teresa. Soon after, the couple went through an *"unofficial marriage"* and moved to a cottage a few miles away. In 1989, Julian, then 18, fathered a son, Daniel, with his "wife" who was 17. A year later, they moved to a rented accommodation 25 miles away in Melbourne and lived there until the relationship fell apart in 1990. Daniel's mother fled with him, resulting in a legal battle for the child's custody that lasted until 1999.

In his early 20s, after he moved to Melbourne with family. Julian enrolled in an early computer programming course through the Rockhampton-based CQUniversity in 1994. CQUniversity Vice-Chancellor Scott Bowman quipped that Julian's passion for *"questioning conventional wisdom"* was supported by CQUniversity's principles. *"One of our core values is openness. You can't get any more open than [WikiLeaks] this,"* he said.[51]

Using Powers for Good as a White Hacker – Truthful for a Good Cause

Julian seems to have had a remarkably short learning curve as a software engineer; because, by the time, he moved to Melbourne with family in the late '80s, he was already widely known as a computer programmer. In Melbourne, Julian was smitten by the counterculture of hacking that was slowly coming into its own. Julian assumed the identity of Mendax, a name derived from *"splendide mendax,"* defined as the art of lying nobly.

Along with two other hacktivists, Trax and Prime Suspect, Julian, in 1987, broke into computer systems in Europe and North America, using *"Sycophant,"* a program written by himself. However, following their

---

51 CNN Wire Staff; "The secret life of Julian Assange;" Indianapolis Recorder Newspaper; Nov. 3, 2011

1991 attack on Nortel's master terminal, the Australian Federal Police swung into action. In October 1991, the police were at Julian's door. Julian eventually pleaded guilty to 25 charges and the case wasn't finally settled until December 1996, when he was fined $2100 and placed on a good behavior bond.

In 2006, he launched WikiLeaks – a not-for-profit media organization for disseminating original documents from anonymous sources and leakers. The same year, Julian penned several essays that reveal a mindset that is in opposition to authoritarian governments sworn to secrecy. It was not until 2010 that Julian became a household name and grabbed international attention when his anti-secrecy organization posted the largest set of confidential documents [almost half a million] ever to be released into the public domain, relating to the U.S. wars in Iraq and Afghanistan, supplied by Chelsea Manning, a former U.S. army soldier.

U.S. Secretary of Defense Robert Gates claimed WikiLeaks' release of the Afghan War Diary[52] could have *"potentially dramatic and grievously harmful consequences."* Secretary Gates did admit that the classified documents did not reveal sensitive information and did not jeopardize sources and methods.[53] In addition, he noted that no one including the cooperating Afghans had been reportedly targeted on the basis of these leaks.

---

52 The Afghan War Diary is the name given to the Afghan War documents leaked and subsequently published by WikiLeaks on July 25, 2010

53 Secretary Gates made his assessment in a letter to Senator Carl Levin, Chairman of the Senate Armed Services Committee on August 16, 2010

On the back of the hype generated by the Collateral Murder video[54] release, WikiLeaks received contributions to the tune of $200,000, which Assange promptly hailed as a new funding model for journalism. The donations couldn't have come at a better moment because Assange was struggling to run the site. In 2010, Time magazine nominated Julian Assange as its Person of the Year, calling him a *"new kind of whistle-blower... for the digital age."*[55]

Wikileaks' entry was a working model akin to a numbered bank account, wherein the identity or face behind the account is concealed behind a number. Working under this cover, a whistle-blower could upload documents to the WikiLeaks site without the risk of being identified and targeted. Journalists could then pick up the information and the system would allow the informant to impose a deadline on the journalist, after which the document would automatically *"go-live"* on the WikiLeaks site.

A Different Kind of Hacking: Neither Black nor White but Gray – Untruthful for a Good Cause?

By 2008, the site had expanded its focus to include secretive religious organizations and cults, besides its routine fare of dictatorial regimes and sleazy big business, because in Assange's view:

---

54 "Collateral Murder" is a classified US military video depicting the indiscriminate murder of over a dozen people in Iraq. The video was released by WikiLeaks

55 Josh Sanburn, "Who Will Be TIME's 2010 Person of the Year?" Nov. 10, 2010; http://content.time.com/time/specials/packages/article/0,28804,2028734_2028733_2028727,00.html

"In every negotiation, in every planning, meeting, and in every workplace dispute, a perception is slowly building that the public interest may have a number of silent advocates in the room."[56]

In March 2008, WikiLeaks posted secret manuals of the Church of Scientology, available only to high-ranking members of the Church, which brought to light some of the strange practices prevalent in this order.

Ahead of the U.S. Presidential Election, WikiLeaks in September 2008, released Governor Sarah Palin's (also the Vice-Presidential candidate in 2008) email contact list, some family photos, and two emails. The personal details were hardly of any relevance to the public and McCain called it *"a shocking invasion of the governor's privacy and a violation of law."*[57]

In January 2009, WikiLeaks published a handbook of instructions of the Church of Jesus Christ of Latter-day Saints a book that sets down basic administrative and doctrinal laws and is reportedly confidential to the mid and upper level male leaders of the church hierarchy. In 2009, a pirated copy of the book *"It's Our Turn to Eat"* by investigative journalist and anti-corruption activist Michela Wrong was made freely available on WikiLeaks, depriving the author of any sales proceeds from book.

On September 1, 2011, WikiLeaks released an

---

56 "Meet the Aussie Behind Wikileaks;" Digital Living; Jan. 31, 2009; http://www.stuff.co.nz/technology/digital-living/524296/Meet-the-Aussie-behind-Wikileaks

57 Michael Shear & Karl Vick; "Hackers Access Palin's Personal E-Mail, Post Some Online;" Washington Post, Sept. 18. 2008

unredacted version of all of the *"Cablegate"*[58] documents. There was widespread speculation that the release of such unredacted data might potentially compromise the safety of informants mentioned in them, many of whom live in countries whose governments are hostile to the U.S.

In July 2016, just days before the Democratic National Convention, WikiLeaks leaked nearly 20,000 emails that had passed between seven officials on the Democratic National Committee (DNC), the governing body for the U.S. Democratic Party, between January 2015 and May 2016. Some of the damaging emails reveal the DNC was actively trying to undermine Bernie Sanders' (one of the US Presidential candidates) campaign during the primary. Following the embarrassing leaks, Deborah Wasserman announced she was stepping down as DNC's chairwoman as soon as the party convention was over.

In October 2016, with exactly a month before the presidential polls, WikiLeaks began leaking personal emails of John Podesta, who was the campaign chairman for Hillary Clinton. These emails gave provided a sneak-peek into the workings of Hillary Clinton's campaign team and discussed key events such as her congressional testimony about the attack on the U.S. diplomatic mission in Benghazi and her paid speeches to major Wall Street banks. In June 2016, Washington Post reported that no less than two groups of Russian government intelligence agencies spent a year stealing DNC's research, chats, and emails.

---

58 The United States diplomatic cable leak, known as "Cablegate" began in Nov. 2010; when WikiLeaks began publishing classified submissions from anonymous whistleblowers

Assange was often accused of preferential treatment of Russia and its president Vladimir Putin. Assange has tried to dodge such criticism saying that Russia, being no more than a *"bit player on the world stage"* compared with the U.S. and China, didn't merit his focus. However, in 2015 WikiLeaks published 11.5 million files called the *Panama Papers* which how 214,488 offshore entities and individuals including three friends of President Putin siphoned their wealth to tax havens.

By early 2012, the U.S. pressure on Assange mounted while Visa, MasterCard, and PayPal had stopped accepting donations for the site for close to 500 days. In April 2012, as WikiLeaks' funds began drying up, The World Tomorrow or The Julian Assange Show – a political talk show started airing on Russia Today starting April 2012, with Assange as host.

The Future of (Wiki) Leaks Journalism

In May 2012, UK Supreme Court upheld a decision to extradite Assange to Sweden where an arrest warrant had been issued in his name after two women accused him of rape and sexual assault. In June, Assange entered the Ecuadorian embassy in London and later in August 2012 Ecuador granted him asylum. Assange and his supporters say they are not much concerned about any proceedings in Sweden but believe he could eventually be deported for political reasons to the U.S., where he could face up to the death sentence.

In December 2014, three of WikiLeaks' staff editors received notices from Google to the effect that their Google accounts had been subject to a search-and-seize warrant from a U.S. district court conducting an espionage probe into WikiLeaks and Assange himself. Internally at WikiLeaks, discontent was simmering especially in the wake of the Collateral Murder video, when Assange became the larger than life "heart and soul of this organization." Daniel Domscheit-Berg, German spokesperson for WikiLeaks quit in September 2010, angered at being kept in the dark by Assange about the secret deals under which several media outlets were given embargoed access to WikiLeaks data. Domscheit-Berg, Assange's one-time right hand, had this to say on the future of WikiLeaks:[59]

> "...every territory needs a visionary to conquer it, and, after the visionary, you need the engineers – and this is the stage that we are at right now. Julian Assange as the visionary behind Wikileaks, and Wikileaks, they have conquered this new territory. They have created a new movement, a cultural change, and now you need engineers that are coming up with very efficient solutions for all of that..."

In April 2019, after seven years of refuge, the Ecuadorean government allowed British police to remove Assange from their embassy in London. While serving time in London for bail violations, Swedish prosecutors reopened their rape investigation and the U.S. Justice Department indicted Assange on eighteen counts related to the release of classified information. While this could remove Assange from the workings of Wikileaks, attention to his plight may draw even more attention to the organization.

---

59 Jon Stephenson; "Interview with Daniel Domscheidt-Berg of Open Leaks;" SCOOP Independent News; March 29, 2011; https://www.scoop.co.nz/stories/HL1103/S00288/interview-with-daniel-domscheidt-berg-of-open-leaks.htm

Wikileaks has earned a reputation for credibility as a whistleblowing site and is known as the gold standard for releasing secret information, but it is also known as a voice for Russia and an avenue for influencing the outcome of national elections. The website points out that it is bigger than Assange, with over one hundred staffers around the world. Never-the-less, Assange remains the face of the organization, and many supporters await the "big reveal" of a Wikileaks without Assange.

Case Study Four

Who's Behind the Guccifer Masks?

Clad in a green prison jumpsuit, *"Guccifer,"* 44, sat expressionless, listening to U.S. district judge James Cacheris in Alexandria, Virginia, pronounce a four-plus-year sentence on him on September 1, 2016. Earlier, prosecutor Maya Song urged the court to *"send a message that computer hacking is a serious offense... He has not at one time expressed sorrow."*[60] The super-hacker, a Romanian citizen, had tormented high-profile U.S. politicians and Hollywood stars by leaking their sensitive emails. His luck ran out on January 22, 2014 when he was arrested by Romanian police from

---

60 Yahoo! News; "Romanian hacker gets 4-year sentence in US;" Sept. 1, 2016; https://news.yahoo.com/romanian-hacker-gets-4-sentence-us-185600637.html

his mud-brick home in a village, 550 kilometers west of capital Bucharest, where he lived with wife Gabriela and daughter Alexandra.

Hacking into the private Yahoo email account of Romania's intelligence chief George-Cristian Maior in September 2013, followed by the over-the-top piece of action of sending Romanian-language messages from that account to Maior's official account, proved the last straw for this *"independent hacktivist."* Blowing his cover – Guccifer, a blend of *"style of Gucci and light of Lucifer,"* the elusive hacker was publicly named by Romania's crime bureau as Marcel Lazar Lehel, a jobless cabdriver and self-taught hacker!

Half-Hungarian, Marcel, is known to have finished high school and hopped jobs, working as a paint salesperson and cab driver, before being out of work for a year before his arrest. He wasn't keen on money and didn't have much in any case. Wife Gabriela says he was unenthusiastic about politics and his only brush with computers was when he worked for a computer factory for a fortnight before being fired. Even so, he is said to be a voracious reader, knows three languages, and prefers the reclusive life in a dusty Transylvanian village caught in a time warp with not even a gas station to its credit.

At 35, Marcel was a late entrant to the hacking circuit and his homespun toolkit consisted of little more than a dated and hulky NEC desktop, with keyboard letters written in orange nail color after the original ones had long since worn off, and a Samsung cellphone. He realized that simply by surfing the Internet, he could assemble a significant body of information on potential targets and then gain access to their accounts through educated guesswork. For instance, he would hack into email accounts by guessing the password or guessing answers to password recovery questions through trial and error.

Marcel pulled off his first series of hacking between October 2010 and July 2011, sneaking into the email and Facebook accounts of Romanian actors, writers, painters, and other illuminati, just to get media attention. To ensure the digital trail led away from him, Marcel struck his victims via a Russia-located proxy-server, scooping out large chunks of their private messages and uploading them to a fake social media account in the name of Micul Fum (Little Smoke).

In February 2012, Marcel stood at the crossroads in life, his ego bruised after law enforcement in Romania had nixed his cybercrime in no time. He could write himself off as a dud hacker and go back to being an honest citizen leading an unsung life. Alternatively, he could rebuild his standing in hacking, this time reaching beyond his small Transylvanian home country, though it was potentially risky. He chose the latter course, and Guccifer, the tormentor of America's most powerful men and women, was born.

In February 2013, Guccifer became infamous with his daring hack of ex-President George W. Bush's emails to his sister Dorothy that revealed two amateur self-portraits painted by the former president. Very soon, he achieved mainstream *"renown"* after gaining access to former Secretary of State Colin Powell's AOL account – by guessing the password from Powell's grandmother's name. Guccifer rummaged around the account and finally came across some messages from Corina Cretu, a Romanian diplomat. Soon he was sniffing out Corina's Yahoo account with expectation, trying out street names in the neighborhood of her primary school mentioned on her public Facebook page in an attempt to answer her security question, and finally breached her account in July 2013. By August 2013, Guccifer had struck *"gold"* by *"exposing"* personal emails:[61]

> Colin Powell's email to Corina Cretu: *"This hacker is driving everyone here crazy... The hacker gets addresses from my contact list which he got when he hacked into President Bush's account. Our security people have been chasing him for months. He may have lots of your emails, maybe not, so best to delete all between us."*

> Corina Cretu replies with irritation: *"I now look like a crazy woman who has been sending you emails all these years like an autist."*

The Smoking Gun website broke the story along with its commentary that the correspondence between Powell and Corina *"would leave most readers with the clear impression that the forlorn Cretu is writing about the twilight of a romance... Cretu calls him [Powell] "the love of her life" and describes a relationship that spanned more than a decade."*[62] Soon after, Powell denied any extramarital affair in a statement to The Smoking Gun:[63]

> *"In light of what was happening it seems*

---

61 Laura Italiano; Colin Powell's email to Corina Cretu: "This hacker is driving everyone here crazy... The hacker gets addresses;" Aug. 3, 2013; https://nypost.com/2013/08/03/inside-colin-powells-hot-and-heavy-e-mails/

62 "Hacker Forces Colin Powell To Deny Affair: Ex-Secretary of State told diplomat to delete e-mails." Auguts 1, 2013, http://www.thesmokinggun.com/documents/colin-powell-guccifer-email-hack-594321

63 Ibid

obvious to ask Ms. Cretu to delete emails... She sent photos on a regular basis. Lots of family photos with her nieces, who she adores, family reunions, formal business sessions, her wedding and some bathing suit photos... Never anything improper... [The two of us] remain friends and are in touch... but have only seen each other once or twice [over the past eight years] at group conferences in Washington, D.C."

In March 2013, Guccifer stole and circulated four memos – relating to the 2012 attack on the U.S. consulate in Benghazi by militant group Ansar al-Sharia – sent to former Secretary of State Hillary Clinton at her private email account by long-term friend and ally, Sidney Blumenthal. Guccifer's 2013 Blumenthal compromise revealed for the first time the existence of a private email server Hillary had set up at her New York home before she took office as Secretary of State. This was two years before New York Times broke the story that the U.S. House select committee probing the Benghazi attack had discovered that Clinton used her own private email server – which *"may have violated federal requirements"* – rather than the State Department email throughout her tenure. Hillary's private email use snowballed into an election issue in a bitterly-fought presidential campaign.

On January 7, 2014, the maverick hacker felt a shockwave speeding from his head to toe after hearing an out-of-the-blue announcement by Romania's head of intelligence George-Cristian Maior. Alluding to the hacker as *"Little Guccifer,"* George announced that America's most-wanted hacker is going to be nabbed soon. George's description of him as *"Little Guccifer"* almost took the hacktivist's feet out from under him because he feared that the investigators figured out that Little Smoke and Guccifer were the same.

Fearing that he was in the crosshairs of the intelligence services, a frenzied Guccifer axed his computer and cellphone into shards and set them on fire in his back garden. Then on January 22, 2014, came the much-flashed images of Guccifer escorted by masked police in Bucharest after his arrest in Arad. Later it transpired that the Romanian intelligence didn't have the faintest idea that existed between the two pennames, Guccifer and Little Smoke, was the same hacker. All the same, the hacking of George's email was a blow to the force's pride, so to minimize Guccifer's stature in the eyes of the public, George had declared: *"Micul [Little] Guccifer will be caught."*

As in January 2014, Guccifer faced a seven-year jail sentence in Romania (the suspended three-year sentence handed down in 2011, plus a four-year sentence for subsequent cybercrimes), which he served until 2016, when he was extradited to the U.S., where he pleaded guilty to a high-profile hacking spree that targeted nearly 100 Americans between 2012 and 2014. In late October 2018, it was reported that Guccifer had been released from a Romanian prison and was ready for extradition to the U.S., much against his wishes, to serve the 52-month sentence.

The Guccifer case is still muddled, and the hacker's motives still remain a matter of conjecture. The most perplexing question is why someone who has already been convicted in 2012, a suspended sentence though it might be, was able to continue to commit the same crime unimpeded at least between October 2012 and January 2014. Viorel Badea, the Romanian prosecutor on the case, told the New York Times in September 2016:[64] *"He [Guccifer] was not really a hacker but just a smart guy who was very patient and persistent... and who wanted to be famous."*

According to the Romanian prosecution, Guccifer failed to dig up anything of a classified nature out of George's email account. From a medical standpoint, authorities in his home country think Guccifer is sane but with a streak of voyeurism as well as an uncontrollable urge for heroism and the associated high. Guccifer would go to any length to suggest he is in a different league from the hundreds of Romanians who join online fraud rings for the lure of earning easy money, saying: *"Of course, I could have stolen money from them. I didn't. Not a single dollar."*[65]

Guccifer 2.0: A Made-In-Russia Fairy Tale?

In late April 2016, the Democratic National Committee (DNC) – the Democratic Party's apex body responsible for supervising its national convention as well as nominating and confirming the party's candidate for U.S. President – noticed something was amiss with its IT network and soon called in private security firm Crowdstrike to identify and attribute responsibility for a suspected hack; meanwhile, the DNC also contacted the FBI.

By June 26, 2016, based on the hackers' distinct

---

64 Paul Szoldra; "The infamous hacker who exposed Clinton's email server is going to prison for 4 years;" Business Insider; Sep. 1, 2016; https://www.businessinsider.com/hacker-guccifer-sentence-2016-9

65 Andre Higgins; "How 'Guccifer' went from online novice to infamous hacker and got caught;" The Sydney Morning Herald; Nov. 12; 2014

signature, Crowdstrike pinned the attacks on two cyberthreat groups, both linked to Russian military intelligence though working independent of each other and without each other's knowledge: Fancy Bear and Cozy Bear. Crowdstrike's security experts reckoned that Fancy Bear must have slinked in during March-May 2016 with the purpose of swiping Democrats' research on Donald Trump. By contrast, Cozy Bear must have been tiptoeing around undetected in the system for at least a year, snooping on internal communications. By mid-July 2016, Crowdstrike is believed to have purged the system of these hackers and its experts stood guard over the network traffic to foil any subsequent break-in.

It was July 22, 2016, when Hillary Clinton was going to be the first woman to clinch the presidential nomination of a major political party in the U.S. from rival Bernie Sanders at the Democratic National Convention in Pennsylvania, that at 10:30 am EDT, whistleblower site, Wikileaks, dumped a tranche of nearly 20,000 emails online, saying *"the leaks come from the accounts of seven key figures in the DNC,"* relating to the period January 2015 to May 2016. Bernie's allies had persistently claimed that the party's primary process was far from open and fair, and the email leak seemed to confirm this fact.

On July 24, 2016, Debbie Wasserman Schultz, chairwoman of the DNC resigned under fire as highly embarrassing emails – like the ones below – released by Wikileaks, appeared to show concerted efforts by the Committee, which should have ideally remained a neutral arbiter in the Democratic primary, to unequally favor Hillary Clinton while trashing rival Bernie Sanders' campaign.

Wasserman Schultz email reply to Luis Miranda, the communications director for the committee: *"This is a silly story... He [Bernie] isn't going to be president."*

Wasserman Schultz said in another email: *"[Bernie has] Spoken like someone who has never been a member of the Democratic Party and has no understanding of what we do."*

DNC chief financial officer Brad Marshall's email read: *"...for KY [Kentucky] and WVA [West Virginia] can we get someone to ask his [Bernie's] belief? Does he believe in a God?... I think I read he is an atheist. This could make several points difference with my peeps. My Southern Baptist peeps would draw a big difference between a Jew and an atheist."*

A flustered Hillary camp mustered enough courage in the ensuing days and Hillary's campaign manager packed more power into that punch: *"I don't think it's coincidental that these emails are being released on the eve of our convention here [in Pennsylvania]... Experts are telling us that Russian state actors broke into the DNC, stole these emails, [and are] releasing these emails for the purpose of helping Donald Trump."*[66]

On July 26, 2016, a pseudonymous hacker Guccifer 2.0 tweeted that he was behind the breach: *"Yeah man ...Wikileaks published #DNCHack docs I'd given them!!!"* On September 13, 2016, interestingly, Guccifer 2.0 figured in the speaker lineup for a computer security conference in London, but actually a *"legitimate"* representative, spoke on his behalf, saying, among

---

66 Jack Heretik; "Clinton Campaign Manager Charges Russians Hacked, Released DNC Emails to Help Elect Trump;" The Washington Free Beacon; July 23, 2016

other things, without any evidence to back it up:[67]

"Who made it possible, that I hacked into the DNC? This is the question. And I suppose, you already know the answer... The real reason voter information became available for non-authorized users was NGP VAN's raw software which had holes and errors in the code. And this is the same reason I managed to get access to the DNC network. Vulnerabilities in the NGP VAN software installed on its server which they have plenty of. Shit! Yeah?"

Guccifer remains very much a mythical character to this day with nothing to indicate that he's for real. He could even be a cooked-up story dished out by Russian intelligence to sow doubts and ensure deniability about their possible involvement. On April 20, 2018, DNC filed a multimillion-dollar suit in Manhattan federal court accusing the Russian government, the Trump campaign, and Wikileaks of conspiracy to disrupt the 2016 presidential election and help Trump win. The DNC infiltration by Russian cyber operatives ahead of the presidential polls, the suit alleges, was part of a broad conspiracy to bolster the candidacy of Trump whose policies were seen to benefit the Kremlin.

---

67 Patrick Lawrence; "A New Report Raises Big Questions About Last Year's DNC Hack;" The Nation; Aug. 9, 2017

Chapter Six

Comet Ping Pong

The Podesta scandal involving the hacked emails of presidential candidate Hillary Clinton's campaign chairperson, released by WikiLeaks in October 2016, contained another chain of events that took social media by storm. This is a perfect example of how social media accelerates and creates alternative reality with unprecedented speed and scope. The outcomes of this can include physical and psychological harm as are illustrated in this chapter.

This is the story of #Pizzagate conspiracy. Hillary Clinton's leaked emails were picked up by users from various forums and dedicated to Trump on Reddit, along with 4chan's[68] far-right fringe message board. Users searched the emails for anything incriminating and came across a discussion that included the word *"pizza"* as well as dinner plans between John Podesta and elder brother Tony Podesta, a lobbyist and fundraiser.

On 4chan, a user made a strange connection between the phrase *"cheese pizza"* and pedophiles, who were known to use the abbreviation C.P. for *"child pornography"* in chat conversations. Somehow, this led conspiracy thinkers to conclude that they were talking about Comet Ping Pong, a pizza chain in Washington. Moreover, the owner of the place, James Alefantis, a fundraiser for the Democrats, was mentioned in Podesta's emails. The conspiracy theory they presented started gaining audience and earned the nickname #Pizzagate. It became so popular that fake articles came to be written about it, and these began to go viral on Facebook and Twitter. These stories directly affected businesses in the neighborhood and bands that had played at Comet's. From C.P., the discussion expanded to include kill rooms, underground tunnels, satanism, and even cannibalism.

On December 4, 2016, Edgar M. Welch, a resident from North Carolina, walked into Comet with an assault rifle and a handgun and fired one or more shots. Luckily no one was hurt. The 28-year-old later told the police that he thought the conspiracy theories doing the rounds about child slaves and pedophilia at the restaurant were true and he wanted to rescue them. After he had satisfied himself that nothing of the sort was happening there, he surrendered.

---

68 4chan is an anonymous imageboard founded in 2003 and has been described as a hub of internet subculture

Even this incident did not stop the effects of the theory, and the conspirators began to point to the mainstream media, accusing it of covering up the incident. They were sure that there was a child-abuse ring inside Comet's Ping Pong. By now, the conspiracy theory had engulfed social media. YouTube video clips started to appear in support of this conspiracy and these videos were viewed thousands of times while tens of thousands of individuals subscribed to the message boards. The conspiracy enthusiasts seem to have worked hard to progress the theories with fake news and crowd-driven detective work. This got so much attention that the police had to release a report refuting the existence of a pedophile ring being operated out of Comet Ping Pong, but the rumor mill continued to grind.

Did you leave a handkerchief?

09-02-2014

FROM: Susan Sandler

TO: John Podesta

The realtor found a handkerchief (I think it has a map that seems pizza-related. Is it yorus?[69] They can send it if you want. I know you're busy, so feel free not to respond if it's not yours or you don't want it.

Source: Wikileaks

09-04-2014

FROM: John Podesta

---

69 Appears in original posting as "yorus"

TO: Susan Sandler

It's mine, but not worth worrying about.

The handkerchief in question supposedly had a map on it, and this was taken as a hint pointing to possible wrong doings. The word cheese pizza has been previously used on 4chan as code for child pornography, and a user guessed that the same coding method was used here. The foods mentioned in the emails were believed to have double meanings as follows:

Hotdog = boy

Pizza = girl

Cheese = little girl

Pasta = little boy

Ice Cream = male prostitutes

Walnut = person of color

These decodes were circulated and the emails with these words were remade and adjusted to include the decoded messages that were intended for the recipient. Here is an example of the type of email that was decoded. It originally read:

Walnut sauce?

04-11-2015

FROM: Jim Steyer

TO: John Podesta and Mary Podesta

Hey John,

We know you're a true master of cuisine and we have appreciated that for years ...

But walnut sauce for the pasta? Mary, plz tell us the straight story, was the sauce actually very tasty?

Source: Wikileaks

04-11-2015

FROM: John Podesta

TO: Jim Steyer and Mary Podesta

It's an amazing Ligurian dish made with crushed walnuts made into a paste. So, stop being so California.

Apart from this, there were also emails between John Podesta and James Alefantis:

Comet Ping Pong and OBAMA...and Podesta?

09-27-2008

FROM: James Alefantis

TO: John Podesta

Hello. Some young lawyer type friends of mine are hosting an Obama Fundraiser at Comet Ping Pong on Thursday Night and then watching the debate. Should be about 150 people and they are raising between 25 and 35 thousand dollars. Would you be willing to stop by around 8 o'clock or so and make a little speech? They (and I) would be thrilled to have you of course. I understand if you are not available.

Also, I saw that you are reading at Politics & Prose soon. What can we do afterward? Would you like to have a dinner at my places?!?

Big or small. What do you think?

Source: Wikileaks

The Satanism factor was also pulled into this whole story with conspiracy theorists alleging that the stars and crescent sign of Comet Ping Pong was tied to that sort of a cult (Figure 2).

On October 28, 2016, a new thread appeared on 4chan – "The calm before the storm," attributed to an

Figure 2: Comet Ping Pong, Washington, D.C., overlain by an image of the devil with alleged similarities circled. The Comet Ping Pong story was reportedly associated with QAnon, a far-right group of conspiracy theorists known for wildly far-fetched plots and falsifications. (image from https://dcpizzagate.wordpress).com/)

anonymous user who, for reasons best known to her/ him, preferred to go by just the letter "Q." What aroused a lot of interest in the thread was Q's assertion that she/ he was indeed some top brass at the US government's Department of Energy, and soon, a whole conspiracy theory episode spooled out; it started to get curiouser and curiouser.

Q would have readers believe that she/he had information on not just how the US administration was run but also specific information on Donald Trump and the Democrats. It was common knowledge that special counsel Robert S. Mueller and his team was formed to probe alleged Russian meddling in the 2016 US presidential election to sway the outcome in Trump's favor as well as the White House occupant's suspected ties with Russian politicians. However, conspiracy theorist, Q, offered a completely different take on Mueller's mandate. That the counsel was actually appointed to probe the liberals and top Democrats like Barrack Obama, Hillary Clinton, and John Podesta, and Trump, without letting anyone know, was covertly helping out Mueller in the investigation based on some altruistic inner call. The other objects of Mueller's probe, according to QAnon, were the Illuminati who have been conspiring for ages to fabricate a new world order and the Rothschild family, easy targets of several anti-Semitic conspiracy theories over the years. Some bakers[70] assume the Vatican's real owners are the Rothschilds! Since the city-state had borrowed some money way back in the 1800s from the family. One baker thread went to the extent of saying that some of NBC "dystopia beat" reporter Ben Collins' scripts were

---

70 The moderators of the QAnon forums and the interpreters of the clues call themselves "bakers," a reference to the "breadcrumbs."

written by Jacob Rothschild, a senior member of the banking family, all of 83 years, and living in UK.

To understand the assumptions held by Q's followers, one needs to first lift the mist around some of the jargon tossed around freely within this latter-day cult. For instance, "Bakers" is a reference to Q's supporters. Bakers carry the mandate of assembling and, in the process, puzzling out the intriguing information crumbs Q "spits out" from time to time into insightful "dough" or "bread," that is, information perfectly understandable for the masses. In some cases, bakers are talked about as "batter," probably in a figurative sense. Crumbs often carry not-so-easily graspable file names called "stringers" which are represented as below:

Helicopter.
CRASH.
Newport Beach.
Hotel GM.
What happened @ these hotels?

_27-1_yes_USA94-2
_27-1_yes_USA58-A
_27-1_yes_USA04
_Conf_BECZ_y056-(3)_y
The_Castle_Runs_RED_yes
Godspeed.

QAnon and its bakers have successfully baked in every possible contemporary happening into their conspiracy mold. In June 2018, Jarrod Ramos, 39, stepped into the Annapolis, Maryland, office of the Capital Gazette paper and proceeded to spray the newsroom with bullets, killing five. Ramos, who had unsuccessfully sued the Gazette in 2012 for alleged defamation had edited a diamond symbol into the pictures of his victims prior to the homicide, and this was sufficient "proof" for many deep-dyed QAnon-ists that the killer had been mind-controlled by the CIA through its MKUltra program. The program was officially halted in 1973, and, none other than the person who headed it, Late Sidney Gottlieb, had concluded that all his work, including on MKUltra, had been practically useless!

One QAnon message seemed hell bent on testing the limits of readers' naivety to no end. It said President John F Kennedy didn't die. Rather, he faked his death, and signed up with Trump's evil fighting organization since Kennedy happened to be a No. 1 fan of the realty mogul-turned-president. Kennedy, it appears, is the one who writes some of the 4chans posts under the pseudonym Q! (That's, too much, man!). Now sample this one, which comes up in the QAnon babble: *millionaire financier JP Morgan sunk the Titanic to bump off some business rivals who were on board!* There is a twist in the script. The Titanic was switched with an identical ship, the Olympic, which had suffered serious damage in a collision, and sunk as part of an insurance scam. Titanic became Olympic and carried on the latter's service.

Either by design or by accident, the information Q "leaks" have turned out to be largely cryptic but, all the same, netizens have instantaneously devoured them. Readers were ready to go to great lengths to pull the multiple cryptic pieces that Q discharged at intervals into a whole. YouTube channels and subreddits within the Reddit social aggregation site that were dedicated to this conversation, came up simply with the purpose of integrating Q's enigmatic information nuggets. The long and short of it is that Q leaks "info" to his/her followers in difficult-to-read bits – *"breadcrumbs"* – simply out of a selfless desire to rescue them from the avalanche of fake news they are caught in. At times, Q pretends he is Mr. Robot, the mysterious and rebellious anarchist in the dystopian drama thriller, and then gets down to the business of dropping crumbs.

The public lapped up many of these stories. One subreddit soon boasted 30,000+ subscribers while QAnon-themed conspiracy videos on YouTube were wildly popular. It was only a matter of time before the conspiracy crossed over from the virtual world to the real one. Diehard conspiracy theorists, notably the likes of Alex Jones who obsessed over and amplified these revelations. Feverishly conspiracy-oriented right-wingers were quick to make connections between white crosses laid down in the desert or painted on the ground outside Tucson, Arizona, as signs used by a Clinton-linked pedophile ring working at the behest of some global elite. Names of movies like Godfather III show up in some of the conversations. The reference to the Coppola film in which the Pope inducts protagonist Michael Corleone into the Knights of Malta order is decoded by a section of bakers as indicative of the complicity of the Catholic Church in the previously mentioned pedophile ring.

The QAnon conspiracy cult and its believers have discovered quirky new uses for old phrases like, say, "Follow the White Rabbit." In their closed lexicon, the white rabbit is a code that, at different times, could stand for Playboy bunny, or Hugh Heffner, or the Catholic Church, or maybe a New Orleans-based Alex Podesta, who is known to play around with stuffed bunnies when not working on life-size sculptures of men in bunny suits. (It hardly matters to QAnon's blind followers that the surname Podesta is the only connection between John Podesta, the chair of Hillary's presidential campaign and our bunny-man artist, and John Podesta's only sibling is Washington lobbyist and Democratic fundraiser Tony Podesta.)

Another usage "Alice in Wonderland" is also popular among QAnon crazies and this could mean either Barack Obama or maybe Hillary is Alice, and the "blood wonderland" is Saudi Arabia. Some mindlessly loyal bakers attribute, without a second thought, the gruesome shooting of 58 people in Las Vegas in October 2017 by a retired elderly accountant as something "definitely linked to the Saudi-Clinton cabal."

When it comes to usage *"Snow White and the Seven Dwarfs,"* not even hardcore bakers are sure who is being referenced. "Snow White" is variously assumed to be WikiLeaks founder Julian Assange or the CIA and spy satellites. There were many conjectures that the seven dwarfs might be the targets taken down by the Storm. The CIA apparently keeps seven supercomputers named after the dwarfs in Grimms' fairy tale. For several decades, starting in the '50's, IBM , the leader (Snow White) in the mainframe computer market, along with seven smaller players (dwarfs) operated computers for several of the US government's alphabet soup agencies.

The Calm Before the Storm

Thursday, October 5, 2017. Location: State Dining Room of the White House. President Donald Trump and first lady Melania pose for a predinner group photo with senior military advisors and their spouses. Even as photographers go about taking pictures and recording video, Trump asked reporters "You guys know what this represents?" and without waiting for them to answer, he continued, "Maybe it's the calm before the storm." One media person inquired, "What's the storm?" "Could be the calm before the storm," was the President's cryptic answer. When NBC News' Kristen Welker asked again about the storm, Trump replied, "You'll find out," without caring to elaborate.

The mainstream media seems to have approached Trump's remark lightly. Meanwhile, Q busied herself/ himself with taking the story in a different direction. Soon another of Q's threads showed up and the loyalist bakers decoded *"the storm"* as Trump's campaign promises. During his whirlwind campaign, the maverick presidential hopeful had vowed to drain the country's swamp of corruption; limit the activities of deep state or a permanent state operating covertly inside the US administration, probably comprising its intelligence and security networks that in the Trumpian view posed a risk to American democracy and threatened to subvert its elected governments; embrace patriotism and resist the globalist agenda of replacing sovereign states like the US with an authoritarian global order among whose aims was to oppress the average working American; and fight a powerful, moneyed confederacy of pedophiles linked to some of Trump's adversaries.

Q mentions in an early post that the depiction of the Illuminati as an eye encircled by rays of light and enclosed by a triangle carries reference to the world's superrich families – the Soros, the Rothschilds, and the Saudi Arabia's House of Saud. Q provides hints that the Soros clan might have sailed past another family to join the top-3 club. Who might that be? The Bush family, the Rockefellers, or the Merkels? Q leaves it that speculation to the bakers.

As per the bakers' narrative, the Triangle is the puppeteer who pulls the strings behind a satanic cabal of countries whose sole aim is to keep the world forever on the brink of nuclear war. This state of suspended animation keeps the world's general populace very submissive to the powers that be. However, to make the warning of an imminent and all-out nuclear war ring true to their subjects' ears, the profoundly immoral and wicked confederacy had to showcase a real threat. The CIA therefore scripted a series of smart maneuvers that catapulted a screwball to power in a hermit kingdom virtually sealed off to the rest of the world – Kim Jong Un. Thus, speaks QAnon. That's not all. The CIA and the NSA operatives are attempting to reveal who Q is, and Q's followers often attempt to flush out the people whom they assume are planted by the intelligence agencies to find out the real identity of Q.

Somewhere in the US, on some cold, dark, and dreary night, if law enforcement were to nab a sadistic pedophile or bust a grotesque human trafficking ring, the bakers wouldn't let go of the opportunity to credit this obliquely to Trump. This was for them, Trump walking his talk, and a sure sign that he had begun to make the wheels of an unwieldy bureaucracy turn faster to deliver on his election promises. This, they believe is going to be an unremitting mission throughout the Trump presidency. For Pizzagate propagandists, this is, without a doubt, the calm before the storm. The Q brotherhood is supposedly informed by some Christian tropes or so its adherents would have us believe. Storm itself harks back to the flood narrative in the Book of Genesis. The time before the storm is called Great Awakening, which is also reminiscent of the evangelical revivals throughout modern American history.

The QAnon community has also rekindled discussions about Operation Mockingbird, a CIA program from the early '50s, which is believed to have engaged 400+ US and overseas journos to carry out propaganda assignments and influence international public opinion. These theorists posit that Washington Post articles about potential Trump-Russia collusion is just another Operation Mockingbird kind of exercise. The attempt to discredit Washington Post comes as no surprise since the paper, along with New York Times and Boston Globe, had reported extensively on how Russian-linked Twitter handles and bots had stoked debates on many divisive issues in the US during the presidential polls to Trump's benefit and even after Trump assumed office. In the wake of the Florida school shooting that left 17 dead, Russian-backed bots and trolls seized on the contentious issue of gun control in the US.[71]

The advent of social media has accentuated the propagation of alternate realities and fake news, and with the enhanced communication capabilities news media brings and the secrecy it provides, the effects have multiplied severalfold.

---

71 https://news.slashdot.org/story/18/05/11/042212/us-congressmen-reveal-thousands-of-facebook-ads-bought-by-russian-trolls

Chapter Seven

Breaking Story – FBI Agent Suspected in Hillary Email Leaks Found Dead!

In June 2018, Neon Nettle, a U.K. website known for inflammatory political stories, released an article on their website that claimed an FBI agent had been murdered at his home in Crownsville, Maryland, as part of a conspiracy to cover up Hillary Clinton's corruption. FBI Special Agent David Raynor, 52, was suspected to have come too close to uncovering the corruption in the Operation Fast and Furious[72] program related to Obama and carried out by the Bureau of Alcohol, Tobacco, Firearms and Explosives (ATF), a division of the U.S. Justice Department,

---

72 https://www.cnsnews.com/news/article/gun-running-timeline-how-doj-s-operation-fast-and-furious-unfolded

beginning in Fall 2009. Under the Operation Fast and Furious program, the federal government knowingly allowed known or suspected gun smugglers to buy guns at licensed firearms dealers in Arizona, walk out of gun shops, then cross the border and deliver them to Mexican drug cartels.[73] The government hoped to identify where the guns ended up and blow the lid on the entire smuggling operations. Some 2,000 weapons are believed to have landed in the hands of criminal gangs in Mexico. Hundreds of these firearms were recovered from crime scenes in Mexico, and the program erupted into a scandal when on December 14, 2010, border patrol Agent Brian Terry was gunned down in Arizona near the Mexican border and at least two of the assault rifles used were traced back to the ATF program but the public wasn't informed of the connection.

Neon Nettle claimed Special Agent Raynor was reportedly *"stabbed multiple times"* and *"shot twice with his own weapon,"* just a day before he was due to testify before a U.S. grand jury that Clinton had acted illegally to protect the Obama administration's crimes while covering up the Fast and Furious scandal. However, Lt. Ryan Frashure of Anne Arundel County Police reported that her officers witnessed Raynor using his own gun on himself on March 7, 2018. Investigators believe Raynor stabbed his 54-year-old wife, Donna Fisher, to death, before killing himself. Lt. Frashure reported:[74]

"There is nothing in the investigation that turned up evidence indicating it's anything other than a domestic-related suicide. When our officers confronted [Raynor], he committed suicide in front of our officers. He was given

73 Ibid
74 Ibid

verbal commands to drop the weapon, and when [officers] were approaching him, that's when he put the gun to his head."

Soon after, the investigators had concluded that this was basically a murder-suicide, and there was an ongoing divorce case between the couple as well as a custody battle over their 10-year-old daughter, apart from *"serious domestic issues."* This could be considered a viable reason for the suicide. However, since this story was out, there was also a special investigation conducted where they looked into the timing of the suicide. It was concluded that there was no evidence to link Raynor's suicide with him testifying before a grand jury either in favor of or against Hillary Clinton. Also, it had nothing to do with the alleged malpractice or corruption in the Operation Fast and Furious program.

Neon Nettle drew the link between Raynor's death and an 8-month-old news article about the shooting of a Baltimore homicide detective, Sean Suiter, 43, in November 2017, using his own gun. Even that article had no mention, whatsoever, of David Raynor, FBI, Hillary Clinton, or even Operation Fast and Furious.[75]

This story illustrates the power that social media has. One article from a disreputable source backed by *"evidence"* from equally questionable websites gave way for an entire investigation.

Time and time again, both in the U.S. election and even apart from it, social media has played a very important role in manipulating public opinion. Using Facebook, Russian and other foreign operatives made

---

75 https://www.snopes.com/fact-check/raynor-died-expose-clinton/

up phony political events in the runup to the 2016 presidential polls. Many people even responded and almost 340,000 planned to attend an event they had heard about just on social media, as per figures by the Senate Intelligence Committee. Ex-FBI agent Clinton Watts, who studies Russian disinformation for the Foreign Policy Research Institute, said:[76]

"Not only did they influence how people viewed Russian policy, they got people to take physical action. That's unprecedented, they just did it persistently, and they did it well."

Facebook and other tech giants refused to disclose a list of the 129 events publicized by the above operatives and went to the extent of downplaying Russian interference in the U.S. election.

Previously, however, they did disclose details about a particular event advertised by Russian-controlled social media accounts. *"Heart of Texas,"* the group they created, publicized a rally that was to take place on May 21, 2016, and gathered people under the banner *"Stop Islamization of Texas"* even as another account, also controlled by the Russians, *"United Muslims of America,"* promoted a competing rally at the same place and time under the banner *"Save Islamic Knowledge."* The Russians, in this case, played both the arsonist and the fireman. They created a rally and then an opposing rally to neutralize the first one, so the intent was that both these rallies would face off against one another.

According to some monitoring groups, in the wake

76 Craig Timberg & Elizabeth Dwoskin; "Russians got tens of thousands of Americans to RSVP for their phony political events on Facebook;" Washington Post; Jan. 25, 2018

118

of the Florida school shootings that left 17 dead in February 2018, Russian-linked bots promoted pro-gun messages as well as messages calling for gun control apparently to sow discord among Americans.

Since there has been speculation regarding collusion between the Trump campaign and the Russians, here is one of the reasons as to why that was brought into question. On August 3, 2016, a group called *"Being Patriotic"* organized more than a dozen rallies throughout Florida state. They bought Facebook ads to hype up a *"patriotic flash mob."* This group even had a large cage set in a flatbed truck that could hold a costumed Hillary Clinton impersonator in prison clothes.

The point of interest here is that the organization of this flash mob was not the brainchild of the Trump campaign, but the Russians. They went all out to stage rallies on the ground, building out on the already hyped-up tension and exploited Hillary Clinton's weaknesses while making use of the ethnic appeal posed by Donald Trump to help him become President.

This entire plot spanned at least two countries and multiple U.S. states, and included all of the above-mentioned tactics to smooth Trump's journey to the White House, according to a 37-page indictment of a notorious Russian Troll farm by the Justice Department's special counsel.

"I hate to say it, but it seems like the creative instincts and the sophistication exceeds a lot of the U.S. political operatives who do this for a living," stated Brian Fallon, a spokesman on Clinton's 2016 presidential campaign. *"There were memes and advertisements that were*

really in sync with the Trump campaign's rhetoric. The messages were in sync, and they certainly exploited some of our vulnerabilities."

"To read about it in this level of detail is pretty gripping," added Fallon – who, like other former Clinton aides, said he was unaware of the Russian meddling as it was playing out in real time.[77]

The level of sophistication that the IRA reached, so they could subliminally benefit the Trump campaign, was stated in the document mentioned above. They studied Trump's campaign and were successful in whipping up social media frenzy to boost Trump's message and show Hillary Clinton in a negative light.

Since Florida was the swing state in the elections and their votes mattered the most, the group of Russian trolls focused their attention on that state, so they could help Trump, as was suggested by someone affiliated with a Texas-based, grass-roots organization.

"Florida is still a purple state and we need to paint it red," the group stated two months later from a false U.S. Facebook account in an effort to rally up real support for its Florida rallies. *"If we lose Florida, we lose America."*

In the summer of 2017, Republican Lamar Smith, chairperson of the House Science Committee, wrote to the Secretary of Treasury that Russia was funding U.S. environmental activism to reduce fracking, the drilling process for extracting natural gas, to stop U.S from

---

77 Ashley Parker & John Wagner; "'Go Donald!': Inside the Russian shadow campaign to elect Trump;" The Washington Post, Feb. 16, 2018

exploring its natural gas reserve to the fullest. The result is that U.S. is unable to supply energy to its European allies and they are dependent on Russia's Gazprom for such supplies. At the request of Chairperson Smith, in October 2017, social media companies provided more information regarding Russian activity on their platforms. In addition, they identified Russian accounts linked to the St. Petersburgh based Internet Research Agency (IRA), a troll farm created by the Russian government specifically to exploit social media to advance Russian propaganda.

On Instagram, Russian operatives shared images on social and political issues related to native Americans, including the construction of the Dakota Access Pipeline. They specifically made it a point to target the *"high visible tension points"* in America, including *"protests against pipeline."* A March 2018 report released by Republicans on the House energy-related panel said Russian-associated Facebook and Twitter accounts were raking up controversy in the U.S. about the environmental side effects of fracking.

The actual findings by this committee are as follows:

- Between 2015 and 2017, there were an estimated 9,097 Russian posts or tweets regarding U.S. energy policy or a current energy event on Twitter, Facebook, and Instagram.

- Between 2015 and 2017, there were an estimated 4,334 IRA accounts across Twitter, Facebook, and Instagram.

- The IRA targeted America since it was well on its way to becoming an energy giant, so much so that Matt Egan of Oil Milestone is reported to have said that US stands to fundamentally reshape the global energy landscape. This was achieved by essentially increased production of natural gas and crude oil by hydraulic fracturing techniques (*"fracking"*). This is backed by the fact that in recent times US has turned from a net importer of natural gas to a net exporter.

- The IRA targeted pipelines, fossil fuels, climate change, and other divisive issues to influence public policy in the U.S.

Many Democrats and Republicans were in unison that Kremlin was manipulating green groups in an attempt to carry out their agenda. The idea that Russia and its government corporations have been funding a covert anti-fracking campaign to reduce the adoption of fracking in Europe and the U.S. has been suggested by U.S. presidential candidates, European officials, as well as the American intelligence community.

Anders Fogh Rasmussen, the then NATO Secretary-General, reportedly said in 2014:[78] *"Russia, as part of their sophisticated information and disinformation operations, engaged actively with so-called nongovernmental organizations – environmental organizations working against shale gas – to maintain dependence on imported Russian gas."*

In a private speech before the presidential elections, Secretary of State Hillary Clinton is believed to have spoken of the obstacles posed by Russian-backed environmentalist groups in the U.S: *"We [the State Department and the U.S.] were up against Russia*

---

78 Mike Myer; Russians Target Fracking, Too; "The Intelligencer." Wheeling News-Register; Nov. 30, 2019

pushing oligarchs and others to buy media. We were even up against phony environmental groups, and I'm a big environmentalist, but these were funded by the Russians to stand against any effort, 'Oh that pipeline, that fracking, that whatever will be a problem for you,' and a lot of the money supporting that message was coming from Russia."

This was backed at a Federal Level by the Director of National Intelligence who released a report that spoke of *"clear evidence that the Kremlin is financing and choreographing anti-fracking propaganda in the United States."* This report revealed that Russian-sponsored news agency RT (formerly Russian Times) *"ran anti-fracking programing, highlighting environmental issues and the impacts on public health,"* which threw light on the Russian government's reservations about fracking and U.S. natural gas production.

A dossier released in June 2016 on President Trump – *"U.S. Presidential Election: Republican Candidate Donald Trump's Activities in Russia and Compromising Relationship with The Kremlin,"* collated by Christopher Steele, a former British intelligence officer stationed in Moscow from 2006 to 2009, alleges a cozy relationship between Trump and the Kremlin.

In a nutshell, the dossier says:

- The Russian regime has been mentoring, supporting, and assisting Trump for at least half a decade to motivate splits and divisions in the Western alliance.

- Both Trump and his inner circle have accepted regular information, provided by the intelligence agencies and Kremlin, regarding his Democratic and other political rivals.

- A former top Russian intelligence officer claims that Federal Security Service of the Russian Federation (FSB), Russia's federal intelligence service, had Trump cornered through his activities in Moscow, and they had reportedly enough information on him to blackmail him. According to several sources, his conduct in Moscow has included perverted sexual acts arranged and monitored by the FSB.

Over many years, the Russian intelligence services had compiled a dossier of compromising material on Hillary Clinton, which contained information, including bugged conversations she had on various visits to Russia and intercepted phone calls, rather than any embarrassing conduct. This dossier was apparently controlled by Kremlin spokesperson Dmitry Peskov directly on Putin's orders. However, it has not been shared abroad, nor with Trump. Russian intentions and plans for its deployment still remain unclear.

Case Study Five

Troll Shop on #55, Savushkina Street

On July 13, 2018, Friday, as President Donald Trump met Queen Elizabeth at Windsor Castle, trouble was brewing back home. U.S deputy attorney general Rod Rosenstein announced at a press conference in Washington that the grand jury for the District of Columbia had indicted 12 Russian intelligence operatives for hacking into the email accounts and computer networks of Hillary Clinton and other Democrats and making off with large amounts of sensitive data. The indictment says that starting in or around 2014 to 2018, the defendants:

"...knowingly and intentionally conspired with each other to defraud the United States by impairing, obstructing, and defeating the lawful functions of the government through fraud and deceit for the purpose of interfering with the U.S. political and electoral processes, including the presidential election of 2016..."

Back in September 12, 2014, the U.S. government topped up its sanctions, first announced in March 2014, running into billions of dollars against Russia, covering supply of goods and technology exports by U.S. firms, U.S. entry visas, asset freezes, several sectors like armaments, energy and finance, major Russian banks, as well as individuals and companies believed to have links to Russian President Vladimir Putin.

How "Translator Project" Panned Out

In April 2014, the Internet Research Agency *("IRA")*, a *"troll farm"* based out of 55, Savushkina Street, St. Petersburg, created a department called *"translator project,"* and by July 2016 there were 80+ fulltime employees. The IRA was reportedly funded to the extent of $1.25 million a month and backed by Concord, a company believed to be controlled by billionaire restaurateur Yevgeny Prigozhin. Prigozhin is widely considered to enjoy close ties to the Russian government

The primary reason for existence of the IRA was to spread distrust towards the candidates and the political system globally. The IRA had many nicknames such as Glavset, Trolls from Olgino, and The Agency, and the organization painstakingly tried to hide its ownership under a spiderweb of Russian entities like MediaSintez, GlavSet, and MixInfo.

The budget for the *"translator project"* was funneled to IRA under the guise of *"software support and development payments"* through approximately 14 bank accounts held by various Concord affiliates. Starting in 2015, IRA and its backers began to open various Russian bank accounts and credit cards in the names of fake U.S. personas. Around 2016, IRA agents used stolen identification of U.S. citizens to open at least four federally insured accounts in a bank in the U.S. as well as nearly five PayPal accounts. Besides, these agents signed up various social media accounts in the names of fictitious U.S. personas and also set up corresponding PayPal accounts for these fake social media actors.

In order to operate cozily from Russian soil, while concealing the country of origin of its disruptive web brigade, the IRA purchased space on computer servers located inside the U.S. The agency set up an encrypted virtual private network (VPN) so that its employees could access this infrastructure from Russia.

The troll farm was effective. Among its many influence efforts, it was able to convince a normal US citizen to stand up outside the White House and hold up a sign *"Happy 55ᵗʰ Birthday Dear Boss"* on May 29, 2016. The trolls convinced the US person that the sign was for someone who is a leader and "our boss." As it turns out, the felicitation was for Yevgeny Prigozhin whose date of birth is June 1, 1961.

John Borthwick[79] studied several incidents of action incitement by the IRA efforts. In one such example, on September 11, 2014, several individuals in and around Centerville, St. Mary's Parish, Louisiana, received a text message that claimed an explosion had occurred at the Columbian Chemicals' plant in the city, hinting that potentially toxic gas might have been released, and in no time the message was going viral worldwide. Simultaneously, the engagement sped across multiple online platforms, assuming the form of a Wikipedia page (now removed) titled *"Columbian Chemicals Co. explosion;"* and a Facebook page of Louisiana News that claimed ISIS had claimed responsibility for the incident. Indeed, the Columbian Chemicals Company, founded in 1922 and acquired by Indian conglomerate Aditya Birla Group, runs a manufacturing plant in Centerville, but all the rest was a hoax.

All the same, the damage had been done. As Winston Churchill quipped nearly four decades before Facebook made its appearance in 2004: *"A lie gets halfway around the world before the truth has a chance to get its pants on."*

Andy Cush[80] noted how the confluence of cyber and classical propaganda used by Russian trolls. In late 2014, hundreds of posters appeared on the New

---

79 John Borthwick used the term "Media Hacking" when describing some of the early attempts of IRA-linked bots to influence actions by spreading fake stories through Twitter and Facebook. These attempts appear to be early experiments to understand the type and intensity of fake stories which could manipulate human action. A complete account appears in John Borthwick; "Media Hacking;" https://render.betaworks.com/media-hacking-3b1e350d619c.

80 Andy Cush, "Who's Behind This Shady, Propagandistic Russian Photo Exhibition?" Gawker, Oct. 10, 2014

York subway, apart from scores of buses, advertising a touring art exhibition in Chelsea, Manhattan. This advertising was accompanied by online blogs as well. The exhibition was entitled *"Material Evidence. Syria. Ukraine. Who's Next,"* featuring large-scale photos that claimed to take an objective look at the conflict in these countries. Later investigations showed that the effort was led by Russian interests. The ulterior purpose of the exhibition remains largely unknown, yet it was used to create an inflammatory show in a high-profile location.

Similarly, in December 2014, Twitter was abuzz with posts about an Ebola flare-up in Atlanta under hashtags like #EbolaInAtlanta, which came from many of the same Twitter accounts responsible for the earlier (IRA-linked) Colombian Chemicals hoax. In reality, there were only two reported Ebola deaths in the U.S. during September-October 2014.

On June 16, 2015, Donald Trump announced his presidential bid, standing in front of eight American flags on a stage at the basement of the 58-storey Trump Tower in midtown Manhattan. The realty tycoon concluded his digressive, hour-long speech on this wistful note:

"Sadly, the American dream is dead. But if I get elected president, I will bring it back bigger and better and stronger than ever before, and we will make America great again."

Almost immediately, the IRA squad was ready for the "kill," with guns all loaded. A Twitter handle *"@TEN_GOP,"* touting itself as the *"Unofficial Twitter account of Tennessee Republicans,"* surfaced on November 19, 2015, and very soon, a Twitter tribe of 100,000 was following it until it was shut down in August 2017. On several occasions in the race for the White House, running up to the election day, Trump's close associates have either retweeted posts or followed @TEN_GOP.

In February 2016, IRA operatives were instructed to *"use any opportunity to criticize Hillary and the rest (except Sanders and Trump – we support them)."*[81] Using previously established fictitious U.S. personas and PayPal accounts, from April-November 2016, IRA started producing, placing, and promoting paid ads on American social media to push narratives heavily favoring the Trump Campaign, sow distrust among communities, and most importantly, spread dirt on Hillary and discredit her presidential bid.

Attempt to Suppress African-American Vote?

In March 2016, a rally was held in Buffalo to protest the death on February 1, 2016, of India Cummings, a 27-year-old African-American woman. She was taken into custody by Lackawanna Police after she reportedly acted irrationally from the use of synthetic marijuana. The protest outside Erie County Holding Center was actively promoted on IRA's *"Blacktivist"* account on Facebook, @NotMyHeritage on Twitter, and RT (the Russian-owned television news network), and mimicked the activism of Black Lives Matter, a movement born in 2013 which held protests against police violence on African-Americans.

81 Tim MUk & Audrey McNamara; "Mueller Indictment Of Russian Operatives Details Playbook Of Information Warfare;" https://www.opb.org/news/article/npr-mueller-indictment-of-russian-operatives-details-playbook-of-information-warfare/

On April 16, 2016, a large crowd was in attendance at a rally protesting the custodial death in Baltimore a year earlier of 25-year-old African-American Freddie Gray. The Blacktivist Facebook group reportedly promoted the Baltimore rally extensively, leaving no stone unturned. One Facebook post screamed – *"Insane! cops pulverized handcuffed man"* in an obvious reference to Freddie Gray's death; another attempted to draw a parallel with one more alleged instance of cop violence – *"Cops raid wrong home and assault pregnant woman."* Baltimore campaigners who had reservations about the out-of-nowhere Blacktivist account were led to believe that the group was fighting for the same reasons as them. On October 16, 2016, the following message appeared on IRA-backed Instagram account *"Woke Blacks:"*

"[A] particular hype and hatred for Trump is misleading the people and forcing blacks to vote Hillary. We cannot resort to the lesser of two devils. Then we'd surely be better off without voting AT ALL."

On November 3, 2016, IRA operatives purchased an advertisement to promote the post of the IRA-controlled Instagram *"Blacktivist"*[82] that, among other things, carried the following message: *"Choose peace and vote for Jill Stein [Green Party]. Trust me, it's not a wasted vote."*

---

82 The "Blacktivist" social media account used Facebook, Twitter, and Instagram to amplify social tensions in the United States. An insightful analysis appears in Donie O'Sullivan & Dylan Byers; "Exclusive: Fake black activist accounts linked to Russian government;" https://money.cnn.com/2017/09/28/media/blacktivist-russia-facebook-twitter/index.html

Islamophobic Content v. Pro-Muslim Messages

Heart of Texas, a Facebook group, announced a protest rally called *"Stop Islamization of Texas"* on May 21, 2016, pointing as evidence to the Library of Islamic Knowledge that opened in downtown Houston a month earlier. A comment on the Facebook page read – *"Need to blow this place up."* Meanwhile, another Facebook group *"United Muslims of America"* put out news about a competing rally *"Save Islamic Knowledge"* at the same place and time. At the rally, both groups had dueling events but neither group realized that both rallies had been orchestrated by IRA troll farm which operated both Facebook groups.

Similar attempts to provoke social groups continued. At a later rally in July 2016, a real American was arranged to hold a sign at the event depicting Hillary and a (fake) quote attributed to her saying, *"I think Sharia Law will be a powerful new direction of freedom."* As election day, November 8, 2016, drew near, United Muslims of America social media accounts spread anti-vote messages such as:

"American Muslims [are] boycotting elections today, most of the American Muslim voters refuse to vote for Hillary Clinton because she wants to continue the war on Muslims in the middle east and voted yes for invading Iraq."

Collateral Support for Offline Rallies

IRA operatives used the Facebook group *"Being Patriotic"* and the Twitter account @March_for_Trump to promote and organize political rallies in New York on

June 25, 2016 *("March for Trump")* and July 23, 2016 *("Down with Hillary")*; a series of rallies in Florida in August 20, 2016 *("Florida Goes Trump")*; and another series of rallies in Pennsylvania *("Miners for Trump")* on October 2, 2016. Advertisements on Facebook were purchased to promote the *"March for Trump"* and *"Down with Hillary"* rallies, and for *"Florida Goes Trump"* events which were posted on Instagram as well.

#VoteFraud Allegations

On August 4, 2016, IRA put out an ad that promoted a post on *"Stop AI"* [Stop all Invaders], a page themed around immigration fears, which claimed *"Hillary Clinton has already committed voter fraud during Democrat Iowa Caucus [in February 2016 which Hillary won by a wafer-thin 0.3 percent against challenger Bernie Sanders]."* On November 2, 2016, the same account hammered home more allegations of *"#VoteFraud by counting tens of thousands of ineligible mails in Hillary votes being reported in Broward County, Florida."* Continuing in the same vein, a tweet from @TEN_GOP alleged on August 11, 2016, that vote fraud was being investigated in North Carolina. However, there have been no instances of widespread fraud in the 2016 U.S. presidency.

False Personas and Email Address

When dealing with U.S. citizens, IRA is reported to have used many false U.S. personas, most notable among them being *"Matt Skiber,"* a fake Facebook name. Matt Skiber, according to media reports, *"contacted"* at least three of Trump's campaign officials; a bona fide Facebook account *"Florida for Trump"* assisting Trump in the state of Florida; and three U.S. citizens to print posters, arrange megaphone, and acquire signs and a costume showing Hillary Clinton in a prison jumpsuit for various rallies. The IRA is believed to have contacted *"unwitting"* Trump Campaign staff as well pro-Trump grassroots groups, using false U.S. personas and emails like *joshmilton024@gmail.com*, requesting signs and placards to be carried at the rallies and their support for the campaign, apart from participation.

Reach of Russian Influence

Russia-linked Facebook posts reached up to 126 million Americans during the 2016 presidential campaign. IRA agents posted an estimated 1,000 YouTube video, 131,000 tweets, and 120,000 Instagram posts. By 2016, IRA-backed social media groups boasted hundreds of thousands of online followers. As an example, the Twitter handle @TEN_GOP had 100,000+ followers. Together, 44 IRA-linked Twitter accounts managed to command a 600,000-strong following.

Post-Election Russian Gambit

On November 11, 2016, a large banner with a photo of Obama hung from Arlington Memorial Bridge in the U.S. capital with words *"Goodbye Murderer."* The following day, IRA organized a rally *"Show Your Support for President-Elect Donald Trump."* On November 19, 2016, it put together a rally titled *"Trump is NOT my president."*

Even as Trump prepared to take office on January 20, 2017, the ODNI published a document on January 6, 2017, *"Assessing Russian Activities and Intentions in Recent U.S. Elections"* with some of these key judgements:

"We assess Russian President Vladimir Putin ordered an influence campaign in 2016 aimed at the U.S. presidential election. Russia's goals were to undermine public faith in the U.S. democratic process, denigrate Secretary Clinton, and harm her electability and potential presidency..."

Special Counsel Investigation

In February 2018, the U.S. Justice Department announced that 12 Russian nationals have been charged with conspiracy to defraud the U.S. and wire/bank fraud. This was the culmination of the investigation by Robert Mueller, appointed as special counsel in May 2017 to lead a sweeping investigation into Russian meddling in the presidential elections and possible collusion between Trump campaigners and Moscow.

Russia Probe: Have Silicon Valley Firms Been Supportive Enough?

CNN reported on December 17, 2018, that the Senate Intelligence Committee was set to release two reports detailing attempts by Russia-linked groups to influence the 2016 U.S. presidential election using Russian social media accounts impersonating U.S. ones. One report accessed by CNN was prepared for the Intelligence Committee by researchers at New Knowledge, a cybersecurity firm, after analyzing a humongous amount of data comprising 10 million+ tweets, 116,000 Instagram posts, and 61,500 Facebook posts by Russia-linked accounts. In its report to the Senate Intelligence Committee, the cybersecurity firm New Knowledge said, without naming any firm, that U.S. social media companies could have provided more valuable data to the committee and also could have presented it in a more accessible format.

Chapter Eight

Follow the (Cyber) Money

New forms of cyber currency have made online transactions easier for everyone. They have also opened up a new opportunity for terrorists to fund their operations. This issue has been highlighted by many, including the former British Prime Minister Teresa May. She cautioned in an interview[83] with Bloomberg that cryptocurrency should be taken *"very seriously, precisely because of how they can be used..."* She was making a plea for stronger regulation of cryptocurrency, specifically bitcoin.

---

83 "Britain should examine criminal use of cryptocurrencies - PM May;" Reuters, Jan. 25, 2018; https://www.reuters.com/article/britain-politics-may-bloomberg-idUSL9N1MY003

Speaking along the same lines as the Prime Minister, the Economic Secretary to the Treasury stated that the government was in talks to amend the anti-money laundering directive.[84] This was a move expected to bring virtual currency exchange platforms and custodian wallet providers within the scope of the EU regulation on anti-money laundering and counter terrorist financing. This came amid growing concerns that individuals are exploiting virtual currency exchanges for money laundering and tax evasion.

The 9/11 Commission Report, the official report of the events leading up to the September 2001 terrorist attacks, states: *"Vigorous efforts to track terrorist financing must remain front and center in U.S. counterterrorism efforts. The government has recognized that information about terrorist money helps us to understand their networks, search them out, and disrupt their operations. Intelligence and law enforcement have targeted the relatively small number of financial facilitators – individuals Al-Qaeda relied on for their ability to raise and deliver money – at the core of Al-Qaeda's revenue stream."*

Using virtual currencies to fund terrorism has not been confirmed to be an ongoing issue, as reported by Europol, the EU agency for law enforcement cooperation, in January 2016: *"Despite third-party reporting suggesting the use of anonymous currencies like bitcoin by terrorists to finance their activities, this has not been confirmed by (European) law enforcement."* If we talk about the near future, virtual currencies may be technically and practically difficult

---

84 "Q2 2019 Cryptocurrency Anti-Money Laundering Report;" CiperTrace; https://ciphertrace.com/q2-2019-cryptocurrency-anti-money-laundering-report/

to use. This is partly due to the fact that large terror networks have already secured funding for attacks such as from remittance agencies in the Middle East. This apart, they are known to prefer simpler methods of funding like getting student loans, which are more straightforward as well as reliable.[85]

Bitcoin[86] can be traced almost as far back as 1982, when computer scientist David Chaum initially presented the idea called eCash in a paper titled *"Blind Signatures for Untraceable Payments."* The entire appeal of cryptocurrency lay in its ability to make a transaction untraceable, which made it a well-known method for militants to finance their activities. Unlike physical money, this is a kind of currency that exists online in digital format. Just like physical currency, it can be used to make instant transactions for routine operations; also, its ownership can be transferred across borders, though its usage is restricted to specific communities. Competing with Bitcoin on the cryptocurrency circuit are others like Litecoin, Ethereum, Zcash, and Dash and, by the look of things, they are taking the spotlight away from Bitcoin.

Cryptocurrency does not enjoy any government backing, meaning that it is an entirely private method of completing transactions. The user doesn't need to produce any documentation to validate his or her identity. Further, in the bitcoin network, users are identified by an alphanumeric value rather than their real names. Moreover, transactions are instantaneous and irreversible. Huge sums can be transferred

---

85 https://rusi.org/sites/default/files/rusi_op_virtual_currencies_and_financial_crime.pdf

86 https://www.thestreet.com/investing/bitcoin/bitcoin-history-14686578

instantaneously from anywhere to anyplace on this planet.[87]

Bitcoin is maintained and operated by way of a distributed ledger, which publicly records every transaction for every traded denomination of this digital currency.[88] The anonymity in a Bitcoin transaction comes from the fact that the user data is not held within the public ledger, so unless one can draw a relation between a Bitcoin wallet(the app that allows a person to send or receive a Bitcoin), and a real person, it is impossible to figure out who owns a specific Bitcoin. In many cases, Bitcoin users, by mistake, expose their IP address to law enforcement, thus allowing them to make the connection between the individual and a certain bitcoin wallet. Ross Ulbricht's is a famous example.

Ulbricht was netted by law enforcement agencies after they tracked the use of his web alias across multiple sites, including Silk Road, an online black market. Soon officials were able to zero-in on his IP address. Once Ulbricht was identified, the U.S. Department of Justice was able to gain access to the bitcoin wallets he had used. As many as 144,336 bitcoins were seized and sold for $48,238,116 as per a court order.

In recent times, many terrorist groups have taken to using cryptocurrency for their transactions, since it is one of the best ways to make transactions anonymously.[89] Since these terror outfits have almost no

---

87 https://economictimes.indiatimes.com/news/ defence/india-needs-to-check-the-use-of-cryptocurrencies-in-terror-funding/articleshow/65290424.cms

88 https://www.lexology.com/library/detail. aspx?g=dff1686f-a927-4d5a-8e05-91e19094e72b

89 http://www.europarl.europa.eu/RegData/etudes/ STUD/2018/604970/IPOL_STU(2018)604970_EN.pdf

official affiliations, it is tough to apply political pressure or the law to stop them. However, new developments are making cryptocurrency more traceable, and security analysts have reportedly achieved some breakthrough in monitoring the movement of Bitcoin transactions, for instance, of certain jihadists. IT security expert John Bambenek keeps track of far-right operatives' Bitcoin activity using Neonazi BTC Tracker, a Twitter-bot software, which tweets every transaction that happens at thirteen Bitcoin addresses typically used by extremist groups (Figure 3).

Figure 3: Neonazi BTC Tracker to monitor Bitcoin transactions

Despite advances in tracking Bitcoin transactions which provide authorities ways to watch suspected terrorist transactions, there are growing ways to keep cryptocurrency movements hidden. One way is to use *"mixer"* or *"tumbler"* services that aggregate Bitcoins from a large number of users and redistribute them. In so doing, these services scramble the trail of transactions, effectively snapping the connection between sender and receiver, to make it more difficult for police to sift the Bitcoin flow. CoinJoin and Dark Wallet are some services capable of adding such mixing services to a user's Bitcoin wallet. Dreaded militant groups like the Islamic State of Iraq and Syria (ISIS) are believed to have employed these services. In July 2014, an ISIS advocate Taqiul-Deen al-Munthir urged ISIS in a blog to make use of services like DarkWallet open-source Bitcoin platform:

> *"DarkWallet's beta release will be published within the next coming months, the mujahideen Dawlatul Islam would simply need to set up a wallet and post their addresses online. Then, Muslims from across the globe could simply copy the wallet address, login to their [wallets], purchase whatever amount of bitcoin they wish to send, and send them over."*

Taqiul-Deen al-Munthir's blog post could well be suggestive of jihadists' aspirations for access to anonymous online financial transfers.

In a 2007 video, Mustafa Abu al-Yazid, Al Qaeda's finance head, even noted: *"hundreds are wishing to carry out martyrdom-seeking operations, but they can't find the funds to equip themselves."*

Several studies suggest privacy coins are being used more frequently by criminals. Europol's *"Internet Organised Crime Threat Assessment"* (October 2017) report showed evidence of more and more criminals using alt-coin (cryptocurrency), particularly Monero, which is unbelievably hard to trace! One of the most notable usages of this open-source cryptocurrency was in August 2017, when the perpetrators of the WannaCry ransomware attack exchanged their illicit Bitcoin earnings for Monero through ShapeShift, a Switzerland-based cryptocurrency exchange.

Journalist and researcher Julia Ebner says: "The high volatility of Bitcoin may backfire in the long run, according to financial experts. Yet neo-Nazis, identitarians, and jihadists aren't short of incentives to invest: they share the anti-establishment sentiment with the libertarians, the desire to make quick money with the speculators, and the need to find alternative transaction routes with the criminals."

Ebner has also stated that since most extremist organizations have had their accounts removed from crowdsourcing services such as GoFundMe or Patreon, as well as payment options like PayPal, Apple Pay, and Google Pay, they are now shifting towards cryptocurrencies. *"They are secure, instant and anonymous,"* said a user on the neo-Nazi platform, Stormfront.

Major terror groups source donations from their advocates around the world, and now cryptocurrency is emerging as a popular channel for fundraising. Take the case of Al-Sadaqah, which ran a crowdfunding campaign towards the end of 2017, reportedly to raise money in support of fighters in Syria. The crowdfunding was linked to al-Qaeda's social media channels and Telegram messenger. Knowing that the campaign might be subject to public scrutiny, Al-Sadaqah restricted the funding to just highly-anonymized cryptocurrencies like Monero, Dash, and Verge. Donations were also collected via Twitter, where they urged upon followers to support the mujahideen in Syria. They also leverage the deep web, part of the internet that search engines cannot find, to achieve their agenda, and because most transactions on the deep internet are carried out using cryptocurrencies, they continue to be untraceable.

In January 2015, Abu Mustafa, an independent cybersecurity analyst, who Israeli left/liberal paper Haaretz identified as an ISIS supporter, was apparently responsible for running a fundraising page on the dark web that yielded nearly $1,000 in donations. The dark web also provides numerous ways of getting things to terrorist groups that are vitally important to their existence. These sites also serve as hidden spaces for the distribution of prohibited extremist literature.

In 2016, Belgium's financial intelligence units reported that virtual currency is increasingly used to pay for illegal goods or services on the dark web, like buying fake documents and airline tickets. These come in useful for terrorists engaged in carrying out attacks on airlines or wishing to travel abroad. In addition, virtual currency is also used to procure firearms.[90]

Al-Sadaqah is not the only militant group to tap into the crowdfunding route to finance al-Qaeda; there have been other cases as well. In 2016, Ibn Taymiyya media center, an online jihadist propaganda unit based in the Gaza Strip, used social media campaigns to raise funds through Bitcoins. In 2015, a Virginia teen posted instructions on how to donate to ISIS using cryptocurrency. In June 2017, the Wall Street Journal reported one instance of a Syria-based Indonesian militant using PayPal and Bitcoins to fund ISIS, as claimed by Indonesian security forces.

In December 2017, pro-ISIS websites Akhbar al-Muslimin and Isdarat were said to be soliciting funds by way of Bitcoin donations. Perhaps a better-known example of the use of virtual currency in recent times is that of Long Island, New York, resident Zoobia Shahnaz. It was alleged that she used virtual currencies to launder $85,000 for ISIS. This may not be the first of such instances but indeed it is one of the most profound, and the trend is expected to

---

90 http://www.europarl.europa.eu/RegData/etudes/
STUD/2018/604970/IPOL_STU(2018)604970_EN.pdf

grow in the future. The U.S. has been at the forefront of the war against terror and has been progressively expanding their anti-money laundering (AML) and counterterrorist financing (CFT) policies.

Now, cryptocurrency remains a minor source of funding for terrorism; even so, there has been a recent spike in these activities, which has been particularly noticed in Virginia, Illinois, the Gaza Strip, and Indonesia. Terrorists may get funding through cryptocurrencies, however, they do need cash for day-to-day operations. For this, they run into the real world "*chokepoints.*" This was apparent from Shahnaz's search history, where authorities claimed to have found search strings like "*ATM withdrawal limit in Turkey.*" Like all new technology approaches, cryptocurrency is also developing gradually, and with its evolution, these chokepoints will disappear.

The threat to the law enforcement agencies and consequently to global security by virtue of terrorists resorting increasingly to the use of cryptocurrency has been highlighted in the whole chapter. Using cryptocurrencies to finance terrorism holds great promise – from the terrorist's standpoint – for low cost, high speed, and verified transactions, which can ensure that several parties, regardless of their geographical location, can work simultaneously to advance their designs.

The use of virtual currency by terror groups exists, at least for now – largely in the realm of speculation. However, there is a very significant potential risk. In the days ahead, if virtual currencies become sufficiently liquid and readily convertible, the risk of such technology falling into the lap of militant groups in Africa and Yemen can't be entirely ruled out.

The onus of foiling cryptocurrency-based terror funding is on law enforcement, intelligence, regulatory and financial services. There are, however, *"lone wolves,"* (a terrorist who acts all by himself and not affiliated to any major terror network), whose relatively small-scale acts of terror can be staged on a meager budget. These funds are small enough to slip through a counterterrorism financing system. New financial technology firms often lack the resources to comply adequately with oversight, while regulators have tended to devote fewer resources to non-banking institutions.

Virtual currencies become a strategic threat in the fight against terrorism, only where they can compete with cash and are readily available at a certain *"scale"* and *"magnitude."* This requires a combination of market capitalization, liquidity, convertibility, and network effects, all of which add up to ease of use.

Currently, terrorists have to make do with the age-old hawala system of money transfer (Figure 4), an informal, cash-based money transfer mechanism via established financial channels. If we look at cryptocurrencies from the perspective of the hawala network, then the threat of cryptocurrencies to launder money on a global scale becomes very real.

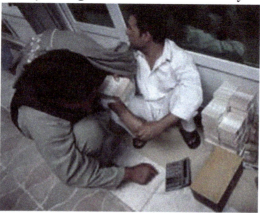

Figure 4:
A generic
hawala dealer
represetnation

Hawala schemes allow terrorists to transfer cash on a global scale outside the reach and scrutiny of the financial regulators while also flouting anti-money laundering regulations with impunity.

There are some interesting similarities between e-gold services[91] and hawala remittance. Experts argue it's only a matter of time before terrorists start using e-gold to finance their activities. They point to a case where both the U.S. and Russian governments were reportedly combing through information to identify a potential terrorist who had threatened to attack if ransom was not paid into his e-gold account. This could also have been achieved using the hawala networks if they used cryptocurrency, and hence, the potential challenge to law enforcement agencies from hawala networks.[92]

Other than the hawala networks, Telegram messenger, jihadis' preferred communication platform, issuing its own cryptocurrency to its investors also poses a potential risk to national security. Once the coin launches, it will be tradable among telegram users to buy and sell services on the telegram open network. The issuing of cryptocurrency by Telegram will make it possible for terrorist groups to easily distribute money, raise funds, and execute their attacks.[93]

---

91   E-gold services allow an individual to open an account in grams of gold and allow instant transfers denominated in gold.

92   https://www.lawandsecurity.org/wp-content/uploads/2017/05/CLSCNASReport-TerroristFinancing-Final.pdf

93   https://www.memri.org/reports/imminent-release-telegrams-cryptocurrency-isiss-encryption-app-choice-%E2%80%93-internationa

SECTION III:

...And The People Who Use Them

Chapter Nine

We Threw a Line in the Water, and Moby Dick Came Back

With his training in the intelligence agencies, President Vladimir Vladimirovich Putin of Russia has been able to convince a domestic audience that he is restoring Russia to the great nation it once was. He has used a multitude of tactics to ensure his continuance in power, and key among these is cyber warfare.

Putin is believed to have made it his top priority to undermine the transatlantic alliance, upon which Europe's peace and prosperity have depended for over 70 years. To accomplish this, he uses the security services, media, public and private companies, organized criminal groups, as well as social and religious organizations to spread malicious disinformation. In addition, Putin is alleged to have meddled in the elections of foreign nations and threatened their energy security, among other things.

Putin owes his ascendancy largely to the general hopelessness that prevailed in Russia under President Boris Yeltsin, resulting from hyperinflation, austerity, debt, and a disastrous privatization scheme, all of which combined to shrink GDP by over 40 percent. At the end of his term, Yeltsin was given the responsibility to choose a successor, and he chose Putin.

The year was 1999. Russia's prosecutor general Yury Skuratov was investigating high-level corruption in the Kremlin, involving Yeltsin's family members, a probe that would result in Yeltsin's resignation in December 1999. Summoned by Yeltsin's chief of staff, Skuratov rushed to the Kremlin, where he was shown a videotape of him in a hotel with two prostitutes. Shortly after that Skuratov submitted his resignation, though he insisted that the *"evidence"* against him had been fabricated. His resignation was still in effect but had to be approved by the Russian parliament's upper chamber, which felt Skuratov should testify first. Just a day before his testimony was to be recorded, the sex tape was played on a TV station after being personally hand delivered by Putin. Later, Putin himself went on TV and told the Russian public that the man in the video was Skuratov.

On December 31, 1999, President Yeltsin resigned, but not before naming Putin acting president. Putin was now the most powerful man in Russia, a role he had been pursuing for some time. To consolidate his power, Putin eliminated autonomous centers of power by reallocating resources from oligarchs to security officers, absorbing oligarch-controlled media empires, and neutering regional power centers that did not respect Moscow's orders. He also began to instate in positions of power former colleagues who had worked in the security services and mayor's office in St. Petersburg in the '90s.

According to a former British ambassador to Moscow, Putin's *"overriding aim appears to be to retain power for himself and his associates. He has no perceptible exit strategy."*[94] The Putin regime has developed a formidable set of tools to exert influence abroad. According to a study by the Jamestown Foundation, these tools include, *"capturing important sectors of local economies, subverting vulnerable political systems, corrupting national leaders, penetrating key security institutions, undermining national and territorial unity, conducting propaganda offensives through a spectrum of media and social outlets, and deploying a host of other tools to weaken obstinate governments that resist Moscow."*[95]

The weapons that the regime used to expand its influence abroad to undermine democracy were first tried and tested in Russia, where laws were passed to hamstring democratic institutions. Russian intelligence had already been working on anti-Western propaganda. However, under Putin, these were amplified. The regime silenced media that deviated from pro-government narratives. They, more importantly, increased the

94 Sir Roderic Lyne, Former British Ambassador to the Russian Federation, Memorandum to the UK Parliament Foreign Affairs Committee, Nov. 22, 2016

95 Janusz Bugajski & Margarita Assenova, *Eurasian Disunion: Russia's Vulnerable Flanks*, The Jamestown Foundation, at 6 (June 2016)

sphere of influence of internal security agencies to survey and harass human rights activists and journalists. Furthermore, they directed judicial prosecutions and verdicts, cultivated the loyalties of oligarchs through corrupt handouts, and ordered violent crackdowns against protesters.

The term cyber, in itself, is not used by the Russians, except when referring to Western or other foreign writings on the topic. They rather use the word *"informatization,"* whereby conceptualizing cyber operations within the broader rubric of information warfare. This type of warfare, however, helps the state get information, which then gives them dominance in all stages of a conflict. This power is needed by Putin's regime, as it constantly faces threats from abroad and within. This vastly differs from the western view of cyber warfare as a domain separate from information warfare and its consequential psychological effects.

Given this ideology held by the Russians, their focus tends to be strategic and long-term, rather than operational or tactical. Steven Blank, a Silicon Valley entrepreneur, is reported to have said:

"While Russian theorists have discussed what they call the information-strike operation against enemy forces, which was evidenced in the 2008 war with Georgia, most actual uses of information weapons in operations have aimed at the domestic "nerves of government" or of society, not combat forces or military command and control. Indeed, the "information-psychological" aspect that covers the use of the press and the media, broadly conceived against

a target's information space, is a key category among many in the Russian definition of IO and IW."[96]

The Russian military has also taken part in cyber warfare, which earlier was exclusively the responsibility of the state's security services. The FSB was apparently at the forefront of coordinating cyber propaganda and disinformation campaigns. The FSB also maintains and operates SORM, the state's internal cyber-surveillance system. It takes over telecommunications, information technologies, and mass communications, as well as oversees the media (electronic and social). They control information blacklists and regulate the media, should their reporting deviate from the pro-government approach.

The agency solely responsible for Russian cyber intelligence, before 1990 was the Federal Agency for Government Communications and Information (FAPSI). This agency, however, was dissolved in 2003, and its components were dispersed amongst the FSB, the MVD (Ministry of Internal Affairs), the Federal Protective Service of the Russian Federation (FSO RF), and the SVR (Foreign Intelligence Service). These agencies were responsible for establishing the parameters of Russian cyber doctrine and for coordinating most of the state's internal and external cyber operations.

The military's cyber remit was limited to areas

---

96 Stephen J. Blank, "Information Warfare a la Russe," in Cyberspace: Malevolent Actors, Criminal Opportunities, and Strategic Competition, Phil Williams and Dighton Fiddner (Eds.), Strategic Studies Institute and U.S. Army War College Press, August 2016, 219-220.

where cyber and electronic warfare overlapped, which eventually changed in the 2008 Russia-Georgia conflict, and even though that resulted in a victory for the Russian forces, it also made apparent glaring operational and organizational deficiencies, including in the area of informational operations. In response to this, the Ministry of Defense announced the rollout of a branch responsible for conducting information operations, which would be assisted by specially trained and equipped troops. According to reports, *"these troops would include hackers, journalists, specialists in strategic communications and psychological operations, and, crucially, linguists to overcome Russia's now perceived language capability deficit. This combination of skills would enable the information troops to engage with target audiences on a broad front, since for information warfare objectives the use of "mass information armies" conducting a direct dialogue with people on the internet is more effective than a "mediated" dialogue between the leaders of states and the peoples of the world."*[97]

Apart from the steps taken by the government to ensure a solid forefront in the military, there are also cyber hacking groups or advanced persistent threat (APT) groups, a crucial part of Russia's cyber-IO toolkit. Even though the Russian government is in denial mode about its sponsorship of hacker groups, the agendas of these trolls and hacktivists seem to be closely aligned with the Kremlin's. Russia is not unique in outsourcing its cyber agendas to hacktivists. China, Iran, North Korea, and others use similar tactics, but where Russia differs is in its degree of success. Russian cyber operations have proven to be so successful mainly because it taps into the country's abundance of technical

---

97 Giles, "Russia's 'New' Tools;" Chatham House, 2016; pp. 29

workers who would otherwise be jobless. According to David Smith, *"Russia is a typical extractive economy that still enjoys the benefits of the quite good Soviet educational system. Great wealth is concentrated in the hands of a few, while many people with training in math, science, and computers look for work. The result is a thriving botnet-for-hire industry."*

These groups, allegedly, on the payroll of the Kremlin, have orchestrated events that are a clear example of Russia's ability to destabilize European powers.

Although the relations between Georgia and Russia were hostile for quite some time, Tbilisi went on to accuse the Russian government of preparing a hybrid battlefield at least a month before Russia invaded Georgia. This accusation was based on the Georgian government's experience of what they refer to as distributed denial of service (DDoS) attacks. As a result, President Mikhail Saakashvili's website was forced to shut down for about 24 hours. Websites of the Georgian parliament, the national bank, the ministries of defense and foreign affairs, and several news outlets were also attacked, even as Russian forces poured into Georgian territories. These two-week long DDoS attacks are thought to have been orchestrated by the Kremlin.

One of the oldest of Russia's cybercrime groups is the Russian Business Network (RBN), which went underground in 2007. Before that, the group was held responsible for more than 60 percent of all cybercrime. Even after disappearing underground, RBN, rumored to have connections with influential politicians in St. Petersburg and Moscow, has been held accountable for numerous cybercrimes, including credit card thefts, extortion, smuggling weapons, drug sales, human trafficking, prostitution, and crimes as perverse as child pornography. RBN's crime portfolio is what prompted Verisign, the internet security company, to describe the group as "*the baddest of the bad.*"

This is perhaps the best time to mention Evgeniy Bogachev, a Russian hacker with a $4 million bounty on his head. According to the FBI[98], Bogachev is the *most wanted cybercriminal in the world.* The hacker is credited with planning significant malicious cyber-enabled misappropriation of financial information for private financial gain. The biggest crime on his résumé is selling malware on the dark web.

The following incidents are a few more examples of malicious cybercrimes carried out by the so-called Kremlin-paid groups of cybercriminals:

- Malware "*Packing,*" i.e., changing malicious software with the help of special software packers, so it is able to evade antivirus software

- Renting out exploit packs, botnets, and dedicated servers

- Renting out abuse-resistant hosting, i.e., hosting that does not respond to complaints about malicious content and does not disable the servers

- Using VPN to provide anonymous access to web resources and protect data exchange

- Evaluating stolen credit card data and services to validate the data

---

98 https://www.fbi.gov/wanted/cyber/evgeniy-mikhailovich-bogachev

The Kremlin uses a wide array of media platforms and tools to craft and amplify its narratives. The main government resources for dishing out information to the public are news programming, RT and Sputnik, which is a radio and internet news network. Both these outlets focus on defaming the west and popularizing conspiracy theories. RT was launched in 2005 and currently reports in six languages: Arabic, English, French, German, Russian, and Spanish. The Russian government directly funds these outlets, and the U.S. Department of State estimates that this funding is almost $1.4 billion per year for disseminating its messaging across media platforms inside and outside Russia.

During the 2014 Russia-Ukraine conflict, RT's foreign staff disagreed with the channel's coverage of incidents, after which, they were taken off the assignment, which was then handled by Russians themselves. A former employee is reported to have said, *"A combination of apathy, a lack of professionalism, and a dearth of real talent keep RT from being more effective than it currently is."*[99]

The Russian disinformation machine doesn't have to be anywhere near to deploy fake news; they benefit from having boots on the ground. Russians often refer to its sympathizers among the political class in the West as *"useful idiots,"* who Russia can count on to agitate against its democratic enemies.

Besides cybercrimes, Russian intelligence schemed several disturbing dark acts during the Ukraine election. The most significant and shocking instance of these acts turned out to be FSB agents' involvement in the

---

99   Giles, "Russia's 'New' Tools;" Chatham House, 2016.

poisoning of Viktor Yushchenko, one of the two main candidates in the presidential race in September 2004. The presidential candidate was poisoned with TCDD, a highly toxic form of dioxin, which nearly killed him. In fact, the toxicity of the poison left his face permanently disfigured. Russian hackers had successfully hacked almost every sector of Ukraine's economy, including finance, transportation, military, politics, energy, and of course, media for three years. Moreover, CyberBerkut, a pro-Russian group that is known to have close ties with the hackers that ruined the Clinton campaign in 2016, breached Ukraine's Central Election Commission website in 2014 to show that ultra-right candidate, Dmytro Yarosh, had won the election. The hackers were also able to breach the country's pension fund, seaport authority, and treasury.

The interesting thing about these cyberattacks was that these were planned to do some serious damage to Ukraine's infrastructure. In December 2015 and 2016, Ukraine's electricity distribution system was brought down by the hackers, leaving thousands of citizens in the dark for hours together. According to Marina Krtotofil, an industrial control systems security researcher for Honeywell, *"these hackers were like street fighters in 2015, but in 2016, they were like ninjas[100]."*

In this day and age, however, Kremlin employs a far less restrictive ideological filter to groom a menagerie of right-wing nationalist groups in Europe and further abroad. These agents can be separated into three groups, according to a study in April 2016, by Chatham

---

[100] Andy Greenberg; "How an Entire Nation Became Russia's Test Lab for Cyberwar;" WIRED; June 20, 2017; https://www.wired.com/story/russian-hackers-attack-ukraine/

House, the UK thinktank[101]:

Major state federal agencies, large state-affiliated grant-making foundations, and private charities linked to Russian oligarchs

Trusted implementing partners and local associates, like youth group think tanks, associations of compatriots, veterans' groups, and smaller foundations that are funded by state foundations, presidential grants, or large companies loyal to the Kremlin

Groups that share the Kremlin's agenda and regional vision but operate outside official cooperation channels, often promoting ultra-radical and neo-imperial vocabulary and run youth paramilitary camps

After a series of revolutions in former Soviet Union republics like Ukraine and Kyrgyzstan, in 2006, the Russian government established the World Coordination Council of Russian Compatriots. This organization is responsible for coordinating the activities of Russian organizations abroad and their communications with the Kremlin. Government organized non-governmental organizations (GONGOs), which receive and disburse funds from the Kremlin, were established in 2007 and 2008 (e.g., Russkiy Mir Foundation and Rossotrudnichestvo). These organizations are headquartered in Russia but have branches all over the European Union and are led by senior Russian political figures, like the foreign minister or the chair of the foreign affairs committee of the upper house of parliaments, while Kremlin-linked oligarchs reportedly sit on their boards.

---

101 Agents of the Russian World: Proxy Groups in the Contented Neighborhood; Chatham House; April 14, 2016.

The Kremlin reportedly spends almost $130 million a year through foundations like Rossotrudnichestvo and the Gorchakov fund. In 2015, it funneled another $103 million in presidential grants to NGOs; the actual magnitude of funding might be higher after including support from state enterprises and private companies.

Chapter Ten

His Button Is Bigger

There was a time, not very long ago, when the world used to laugh at North Korean cyber power. Well, they don't laugh at it anymore. We have grown up in a world where North Korea is considered an arsenal-craving country ruled by cartoonish despots. The fact that few people know is that the North Korean regime is morphing into a modern version of authoritarianism, which, according to Dylan Stent, an expert on national security in the Korean Peninsula, comes with cyberwar capabilities that complement hydrogen bombs! Stent goes on to say that it's always the nukes that catch the world's attention, but the North Korean regime is also growing at an unprecedented pace in the cyber domain.

In the past few years, North Korea's hacking competence has increased exponentially. In 2017, the country's missile and nuclear proliferation made headlines across the globe, while its professionally trained hackers quietly honed their cyber capabilities.

What went largely unnoticed was that by 2013, North Korean agents had compromised a major chunk of South Korea's banking system. In 2016, the Lazarus Group, linked to North Korean cybercrime groups, was accused of hacking the Central Bank of Bangladesh and stealing $851 million, a heist carried out through the Federal Reserve Bank in New York. Using the Swift messaging system, the hackers convinced the Federal Reserve Bank to transfer the sum to a North Korean-controlled account in the Philippines. But for a spelling error, the hackers would have quietly pocketed almost $1 billion. The bankers grew suspicious when they received a withdrawal request with *"foundation"* misspelt as *"fandation."*

But that was just a beginning. The North Korean cybercrimes only got better with time. Last year, the world came to a temporary halt when WannaCry virus infected millions of computers. This chapter explores the cyber power of North Korea and sheds light on how it continues to develop with time.

Rise of North Korean Cyber Power

North Korea experienced a surge of cyber power in 1994, the year when Kim Jong-Il inherited the leadership from his father Kim Il-sung. That was also the time when North Korea was in desperate need of hard currency as the country suffered from severe flooding and was cut off from trade as a result of the Cold War. In order to stand the country back on its feet, the younger Kim appeared to have thought of cybercrimes as a revenue source. Soon cyber training started at some of the most prestigious universities in Pyongyang. Trained hackers were posted overseas, including in China and other Southeast Asian countries, and given targets of $100,000 every year!

Ninety percent of the money extracted from cyber-attacks was siphoned off to the Pyongyang regime. According to Bloomberg's Sam Kim, these large sums were raised by pirating different software and selling it online to Korean and Chinese customers as well as from gambling, hacking, and gaming websites. It is assumed that China was complicit in helping North Korea carry out these activities.

> *"The U.S. Department of Defense states that North Korean intelligence and security services collect political, military, economic, and technical information through open-source, human intelligence, cyber, and signals intelligence capabilities. North Korea's primary intelligence collection targets remain South Korea, the United States, and Japan."[102]*

North Korea's cyber capabilities were modernized in 2009 with the inauguration of the Reconnaissance General Bureau (RGB), the country's primary foreign intelligence service, responsible for carrying out clandestine cyber-attacks as prescribed by the state. The RGB is considered to have six bureau's or operational units. However, the terms "bureau," "The Bureau," and "Lazarus Group" are used synonymously to indicate the

---

102 Stent, D., "The Great Cyber Game: Dylan Stent Discusses North Korea's Cyber Strategy in the 21st Century," *New Zealand International Review*, September-October 2018.

sophistication of the cyber capability in North Korea.

North Korea is light years away from being able to spend the kind of money that countries like the U.S., China, Japan, and South Korea spend on military and technology. Thus, the only viable option for North Korea is to divert its resources to cybercrime if it wants to compete with the developed world.

According to Chris Inglis, a former deputy director of the National Security Agency, who now teaches security at the U.S. Naval Academy:

> *"Cyber is a tailor-made instrument of power for North Korea. There's a low cost of entry, it's largely asymmetrical, there's some degree of anonymity and stealth in its use. It can hold large swaths of nation-state infrastructure and private-sector infrastructure at risk. It's a source of income."[103]*

To pull off successful cyber intrusions, all it takes is a fast internet connection and some training. North Korea has built up an arsenal of 6,000 trained hackers, all serving its military, according to a North Korean defector who spoke to the BBC. The unnamed defector who used to teach computer science at a reputed Pyongyang university claimed that many of his students were given tasks related to hacking at Bureau 121![104]

---

103 Sanger, D., Kirkpatrick, D. & Perlroth, N., The World Once Laughed at North Korean Cyberpower. No More, The New York Times, October 15, 2017, https://www.nytimes.com/2017/10/15/world/asia/north-korea-hacking-cyber-sony.html

104 Bureau 121 and No. 91 Office are considered to be latest additions to the bureau's under RGB.

North Korea is the least wired country in Asia with only a few IP addresses and limited internet traffic but that is no reason to underestimate its power to disrupt the cyber world. McAfee, in its report entitled, "A Map of the Most Dangerous Sources of Cybercrime," reported that after Russia, North Korea is the next most capable country when it comes to carrying out cybercrimes and that the Reconnaissance General Bureau has stolen tens of millions of dollars from banks in developing countries, which has provided a lucrative way to supplement the North Korean government's access to foreign currency.[105]

The Lazarus Connection

It was Symantec that drew the world's attention for the first time to the Lazarus Group. Lazarus happens to have several offshoots like Bluenorroff, which trains its cyber-attacks on foreign financial institutions, the culprit in the Bangladesh Bank heist, and the very recent mining[106] of Monero cryptocurrency in developing countries.

Andariel is another outgrowth of the Lazarus Group, and its theater of action is South Korea, where it is known to have targeted huge conglomerates and the defense industry for the purpose of espionage and profiteering. Andariel was responsible for the 2016 South Korean Cyber Center attack, in which North Korea's intelligence stole 235 GB of classified US and

---

105 McAfee, "A Map of the Most Dangerous Sources of Cybercrime" (https://securingtomorrow.mcafee.com/ business/map-dangerous-sources-cybercrime/).

106 "Mining" of crypt currency is the process of computers solving complex math problems to create a new digital coin.

South Korean military plans[107]. The US Department of Treasury announced sanctions against Andariel in 2019 for "... attempting to steal bank card information by hacking into ATMs to withdraw cash or steal customer information to later sell on the black market. Andariel is also responsible for developing and creating unique malware to hack into online poker and gambling sites to steal cash.[108]

Cyber espionage by North Korea commenced in 2009 when the bureau (RGB) was formed. The McAfee Group unveiled a domestic espionage campaign and called it "Operation Troy," geared towards gathering information about South Korean military.

In 2009, the bureau stole confidential documents containing details of South Korea's response in the event of an attack, including chemical warfare, by the North. From 2009 to 2013, the bureau has been reported to deploy malware in South Korean military networks capable of exfiltrating classified information.

In 2017, North Korean hackers reportedly ripped off gigabytes of cached data relating to South Korean military assets. The booty included detailed wartime contingency plans prepared by South Korea in collaboration with the U.S. In the same year, North Korean hackers broke into South Korea's cyber command.

---

107 Two plans which were stolen have been revealed. First, how the South would respond to a strike by North's commandos. And, second, how a "decapitation strike" could take place by the South which would specifically target North's key govt. officials. The details of other data are still unknown.

108 US Department of the Treasury; "Treasury Sanctions North Korean State-Sponsored Malicious Cyber Groups;" Sept. 13, 2019.

North Korea and Worldwide Cyber Disruption

In 2009, North Korea launched a cyber-attack on both U.S. and South Korea in response to U.N. sanctions after Pyongyang conducted a nuclear weapon test earlier that year. In what is considered as North Korea's first DDOS (Distributed Denial of Service) attack, hackers flooded government and private networks in the U.S. and South Korea with millions of requests from computers infected with *"MyDoom,"* a North Korean botnet virus. Anti-terrorism expert Richard A. Clark[109] considered the attack as equivalent to waging war on both these countries. In the U.S., this botnet virus affected the networks of the Department of State, National Security Agency, White House, Department of Homeland Security, NASDAQ, Yahoo.com, Amazon. com, and the New York Stock Exchange. In South Korea, it crippled the networks of South Korea's Presidential Office, National Intelligence Service, National Assembly, Chosun news site, Ministry of National Defense, Korea Exchange Banks, and AhnLab, a leading network security firm.

One of the startling cyber-attacks by North Korea came in March 2013. During this incident, North Korean hackers were able to freeze the computer networks of three major South Korean banks and render ATMs inoperable.

North Korean Cyber-Attack on Sony Pictures Entertainment

In 2014, Sony Pictures Entertainment was about

---

109 Author Interviews; "Richard Clarke On The Growing 'Cyberwar' Threat;" Apr. 19, 2010; https://www.npr.org/transcripts/126097038

to release "The Interview," a comedy starring James Franco and Seth Rogen, whose plot revolved around assassinating Kim Jong-un, North Korea's leader. North Korea initially issued a number of threats, warning Sony to cancel the release. Eventually, North Korean agents hacked Sony Pictures' IT infrastructure and revealed sensitive and confidential information pertaining to its employees. Following threats to moviegoers, Sony canceled the theatrical release of the movie though it still managed to release the movie online on YouTube and other streaming sites.

The information leaked by the North Korean hacking group included a series of private emails exchanged between Amy Pascal, then co-chair of Sony, and Scott Rudin, film producer. The emails saw the pair indulging in casual and rather insensitive racist speculation about what might have been Barrack Obama's favorite films during the previous year. Needless to say, the duo focused mostly on films starring and about African Americans.

North Korean Cyber-Attack on Bangladesh Bank

In September 2018, the U.S. Justice Department accused a North Korean spy, Park Jin Hyok, of carrying out high-profile cyber-attacks, including the Bangladesh Bank hack. Park's cybercrime was apparently sponsored by North Korea's dreaded Lazarus Group, the same hacking team responsible for the 2017 WannaCry 2.0 ransomware attack and the attack on Sony hack in 2014. The Department of Justice claimed that using the same methods, the same set of hackers also managed to hack several other banks in Vietnam, Africa, Southeast Asia, and the Philippines from 2015 through 2018. The heist is believed to be to the tune of $1 billion!

In the criminal complaint unsealed against Park Jin Hyok, Assistant Attorney General Demers noted, "The complaint alleges that the North Korean government, through a state-sponsored group, robbed a central bank and citizens of other nations, retaliated against free speech from way across the globe, and created disruptive malware that indiscriminately affected victims in more than 150 other countries, causing hundreds of millions, if not billions, of dollars' worth of damage."[110]

In September 2018, Park was charged with two counts of crime – namely committing computer abuse and fraud and conspiracy to commit wire fraud – which together carry a maximum prison term of 25 years.

Cyber-Attacks Are Cost-Effective and Deniable for North Korea

The U.S. Department of Defense said in a report presented to Congress[111] that North Korea views cyber as a cost-effective, deniable, and asymmetric tool that the country can use to its advantage as and when it wants, without having to fear any reprisal attacks. The reason why North Korea is able to carry out cybercrimes so easily is that its networks are separated from the internet. The country most likely piggybacks on the internet infrastructure of third-party nations and

---

110 The United States Department of Justice; "North Korean Regime-Backed Programmer Charged With Conspiracy to Conduct Multiple Cyber Attacks and Intrusions;" Sept. 6, 2018. https://www.justice.gov/opa/pr/north-korean-regime-backed-programmer-charged-conspiracy-conduct-multiple-cyber-attacks-and

111 Office of the Secretary of Defense; "Military and Security Developments Involving The Democratic People's Republic of Korea; No. 9-600987B; 2017."

remain hidden as a perpetrator in this process.

According to South Korean vice foreign minister Ahn Chong-ghee, "North Korea has been blatantly carrying out cyber-attacks through third world countries in order to cover up the origin of the attacks."[112]

North Korea is also accused of staging a sophisticated cyber-attack on the South Korean nuclear reactor in 2014. However, the country denied any involvement in the attack, which was controlled apparently from a base in China.[113] The attack resulted in the leak of personal details of 10,000 KHNP workers, designs and manuals for at least two reactors, electricity flow charts, and estimates of radiation exposure among local residents. There was no evidence, however, that the nuclear control systems had been hacked.

The Malaysia Connection

The concept Malaysia is a base of choice for North Korean hackers often goes unnoticed, according to Yoo Dong-ryul,[114] a former South Korean police researcher who has closely studied North Korean espionage techniques for at least 25 years. He claims that there are two Malaysian IT firms enjoying close ties with RGB. However, the involvement of these companies in any cyber-attack has so far not been established.

---

112   Reuters; "Inside The Elite North Korean Cyber Warfare Cell Behind the Sony Hack: Report;" May 21, 2017; https://finance.yahoo.com/news/inside-elite-north-korean-cyber-132004050.html

113 The Guardian; "South Korean nuclear operator hacked amid cyber-attack fears;" Dec. 23, 2014.

114 Ju-min Park & James Pearson; "North Korea's Unit 180, the cyber warfare cell that worries the West;" Reuters; May 20, 2017.

Kaspersky Lab Results

After investigating the Lazarus Group for over a year, Kaspersky Lab was able to uncover the tools used by the group and construct its modus operandi[115]:

- The first stage is *Initial Compromise*, where a single security system in a bank is breached either with a remotely accessible vulnerable code, i.e., on a web server or through a watering hole attack[116], with the help of an exploit planted on a benign website. Once this website is visited, the bank employee's computer gets the malware.

- The second stage is called *Foothold Established*. The hacking group migrates to several other bank hosts in order to deploy persistent backdoors. The malware allows the hackers to log in and log out whenever they want.

- *Internal Reconnaissance* is the third stage. In this stage, the hacking group spends weeks or even months to study the network and identify valuable resources, such as the backup server, which store all the authentication data. Another resource that the hacking group tries to learn about is a mail server or the whole domain controller that will help the group gain access to every server that stores and processes records of financial transactions.

---

115   Kaspersky   Lab,   https://www.kaspersky.com/about/press-releases/2017_chasing-lazarus-a-hunt-for-the-infamous-hackers-to-prevent-large-bank-robberies

116 A "Watering Hole Attack" is a computer attack strategy of infecting a web site visited by a target with malware. Eventually as members of the target organization visit this site; they, too, get infected.

- The fourth and last stage is dubbed *Deliver and Steal*. This is where the hackers deploy special malware capable of circumventing the internal security features of the financial software to make rogue transactions on behalf of the bank.

Kaspersky Lab found more than 150 malware samples relating to the Lazarus Group's recent activities in financial institutions, investment companies, and swaths of cryptocurrency businesses across several countries such as India, South Korea, Bangladesh, Vietnam, Indonesia, Costa Rica, Poland, Malaysia, Iraq, Ethiopia, Nigeria, Kenya, Gabon, Uruguay, and Thailand. The most recent malware samples were detected in March 2017. Kaspersky Lab also revealed that the Lazarus Group was responsible for the Bangladesh bank hack.

The Lazarus Group is known for investing heavily in the latest variants of the malware they frequently use. For months, the group was trying to make a tool set that would be invisible to all security solutions. Fortunately, Kaspersky Labs has been keeping track of all the new malware samples; thus, forcing the Lazarus Group to rework their arsenal. Kaspersky Lab published a report of their one yearlong effort into the activities of Lazarus beginning with their theft of 82 million dollars from the Central Bank of Bangladesh.

While they reported that the group had been quiet since the theft, they also stated that: "We're sure they'll come back soon. In all, attacks like the ones conducted by Lazarus group show that a minor misconfiguration may result in a major security breach, which can potentially cost targeted business hundreds of millions of dollars in loss."

How to Counter the Cyber-Attacks Perpetrated by North Korea

Most likely, the Kim regime believes that North Korea can win back the same tactical balance of power the country had during the '50s if it continues to threaten the world and keep on orchestrating frequent disruptions in the cyber world. As it turns out, the cyber capabilities of North Korea have flaws as well. For instance, in 2014, as a retaliation to the Sony hack, the U.S. hit back at Pyongyang with a lethal DDOS attack that sent Kwangmyong, the renegade nation's intranet service, offline, and exposed North Korea's cyber vulnerabilities. North Korea's cyber operability is likely supported by infrastructure and access provided by Chinese government. Should Beijing reduce/stop supporting North Korea cyber operations, North Korean operations will be severely marginalized.

Case Study Six

Hacked by *"Guardians of Peace:"* Sony Pictures Entertainment

On Monday, November 24, 2014, the first thing that met the eyes of staff at Sony Pictures Entertainment (SPE) headquarters in Culver City, California, as they tried to log on to their work computers, was the image of a smirking red skeleton with the following message: *"Hacked by #GOP"* (apparently short for *"Guardians of Peace,"* a hitherto anonymous group). By 10:50 am the same day, the news broke that Sony Pictures network and computers had been hacked. The hideous screenshot was posted on Reddit news aggregation site by a user who claimed to be an ex-SPE employee. The user reported that the screen shot was on every computer at the entertainment company (Figure 5).

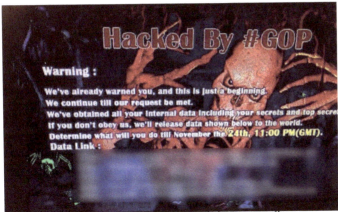

Figure 5: The Guardians of Peace warning screen (image publicly available)

The hackers had ripped off some 100 terabytes of data. For comparison, the entire digitized content of the American Library of Congress is around 10 terabytes. With the company's computer network compromised, many computers disabled, and employees' workflow upset, SPE was reportedly running business like in the old days with pen, paper, land phones, whiteboard, and fax, amidst fears that data might be lost or stolen.

Soon after, DVD copies, many of which were watermarked, of five new SPE movies – Still Alice, Mr. Turner, Annie, Fury, and To Write Love on Her Arms – appeared online within minutes of each other. Meanwhile, someone claiming to be the *"boss of GOP"* emailed various media outlets saying the group was behind the leak of upcoming SPE movies.

The FBI began an investigation of the SPE hack amidst speculation that North Korea might have orchestrated the hack. The hack was thought to be in retaliation for the release of the movie, "The Interview," a satirical comedy distributed by Columbia Pictures, an SPE division. The movie featured James Franco and Seth Rogen as bumbling idiots tasked by the CIA to eliminate North Korean leader Kim Jong-un by exposing him to a deadly toxin.

In the wake of the SPE hack, North Korea denied all involvement in the incident, and its diplomats quickly labelled the hacking as another fabrication targeting their government. Even so, on December 7, 2014, a North Korean source was quoted as saying that the country had a great number of supporters and sympathizers all over the world who may have carried out the attack and reportedly praised the hack as a righteous deed. Even as the FBI was on the case, SPE hired SealMandiant, a cyber-security firm *to* clean up the attack and remove any remining malware from its network.

Leaked documents from the studio also started to surface online, some of which showed SPE in a very unflattering light. In an industry where compensation is a closely-held secret, a spreadsheet from the hack revealed that 17 of the top SPE executives were in the $1-million club. It's CEO Michael Lynton and co-chair Amy Pascal both took home $3 million annually. Amy was the only woman in this august society at the helm. Other instances of gender pay gap were noted by readers of leaked documents, such as Hannah Minghella, president of production at Columbia Pictures, an SPE unit, earned nearly 1 million dollars less than Michael De Luca, another executive with the same job title. One commentator who fine-combed the leaked document quipped that the *"upper echelons of Sony Pictures"* was 94 percent male and 88 percent white.

The spreadsheet also gave away compensation data of 6,000 SPE staff, including details of current salaries, bonus plans, job titles, and even home addresses. In addition, by mid-December 2014, the hackers had released a monstrous 150 gigabytes of sensitive, kick-in-the-teeth and at times rib-tickling emails, as well as internal financial stats, passports, and visas of cast and crew members, confidential contracts, employee social security numbers, and medical records.

On December 2, nine days after the breach, SPE top guns, Michael Lynton and Amy Pascal provided the following alert to all of their staff:

> *"It is now apparent that a large amount of confidential Sony Pictures Entertainment data has been stolen by the cyber attackers, including personnel information and business documents. While we are not yet sure of the full scope of information that the attackers have or might release, we unfortunately have to ask you to assume that information about you in the possession of the company might be in their possession...[117]"*

Another file that surfaced on December 3, with a seemingly innocent title *"Sony_2012_Comment"* is a virtual pile upon pile of employee rants about how awful work in the struggling studio is, as evidenced by the following samples[118]:

> *"Seems like we just reboot old product instead of coming up with new ideas like the Hunger Games. We need new fresh ideas that can drive*

117 Saba Hamedy, "Sony tries to contain damage as hackers leak more data;" Los Angeles Times, Dec. 4, 2014.

118 Sam Biddle; "Sony Hack Reveals 25-Page List of Reasons It Sucks To Work at Sony;" Dawker, Dec. 3, 2014. The entire library of Sony documents is available at the WikiLeaks site.

franchise product. Go out and hire the best."

"There is a general 'blah-ness' to the films we produce. Although we manage to produce an innovative film once in a while, Social Network, Moneyball, The Girl with the Dragon Tattoo, we continue to be saddled with the mundane, formulaic Adam Sandler films... We only release a dozen or so Columbia Pictures a year, for example. And will we still be paying for Adam Sandler Why?... The studio needs to change deal structure that has been in place with Happy Madison as this arrangement has disproportionately benefitted Adam Sandler and his team, relative to SPE."

"Upper management allows certain talent and filmmakers to bleed us dry with their outlandish requests for private jets, wardrobe and grooming stylists – and are surprised when they are asked to work more than 5 hours to promote their film."

"Are you aware that Men in Black 3 may gross $600M at the box office, and yet will lose money for SPE? Shouldn't we question that strategy?... Have you read the SEC annual report? Disney will make $300M on Spidey merchandise this year alone. We won't! ... Stop making the same, safe, soul-less movies and TV shows. Enough with the remakes and reboots."

The worst part of the hack was how SPE made the job of the hackers easy, by reportedly storing thousands of private passwords in plaintext unprotected files, many of which were associated with key financial and corporate voicemail accounts. Cybersecurity experts from Trend Micro also identified similarities between the malicious code used in the SPE breach and the March 2013 Dark Seoul attack that infected six organizations in South Korea.

The cyberattack erased data, including confidential communication from as much as 50 percent of SPE's personal computers and servers and left the studio with just 30 percent of its computing capability. Security researchers believed that SPE would need to spend at least $80 million to recover from the breach. Mandiant chief Kevin Mandia reported to CEO Michael:

> *"The scope of this attack differs from any we have responded to in the past, as its purpose was to both destroy property and release confidential information to the public. The bottom line is that this was an unparalleled and well-planned crime carried out by an organized group[119]."*

In all, more than 170,000 pieces of digital correspondence between SPE executives like Michael Lynton and Amy Pascal, and former Motion Picture Group executives like Scott Rudin and Rooney Mara, were leaked online and are not archived in searchable form on the WikiLeaks websites. Several magazines have reported "interesting" observations based on this data. For example, The Wrap, published what it called the "Greatest Hits of Leaked Sony Emails: Angelina Jolie, "Aloha," David Fincher and More, in which it noted the following:

1. Film and theater producer Scott Rudin tells Amy: *"I'm not destroying my career over a minimally talented spoiled brat [actress Angelina Jolie]*

---

119 Sam Frizell; "Internal Memo: Sony Could Not Have Prepared For 'Unprecedented' Hack;" Time; Dec. 8, 2014.

who thought nothing of shoving this off her plate for eighteen months so she could go direct a movie. ...She's a camp event and a celebrity and that's all..."

2. Amy to Scott Rudin: *"What should I ask the president [Barack Obama] at this stupid Jeffrey breakfast?"*

Scott: *"Would he like to finance some movies?"*

Amy: *"I doubt it. Should I ask him if he liked Django?"*

Scott responds: *"12 YEARS [12 Years a Slave (2013)]"*

Amy: *"Or the butler [The Butler (2013)]. Or think like a man? [sic]"*

Scott: *"Ride-along. I bet he likes Kevin Hart."*

3. Amy asks Cameron Crowe if he had something to show her that particular week. To this, the director of "Almost Famous" responds: *"Does Bruce Jenner [Caitlyn Jenner] want boobs? Hell yes, I have something to show you!!!!"*

4. SPE's president of production Michael De Luca writes: *"He [Fassbender] just makes you feel bad to have normal-sized genitalia."*

5. An enraged Amy writes to Scott: *"He [screenwriter-director Aaron Sorkin] is broke. He wants to get paid... We paid him his insane fee [for some work he had done] on Flash Boys... When the poker movie [Molly's Game] came around [,] we didn't want to not be in the Aaron business, so we wanted that too... I don't care if Aaron is sleeping with the girl or not..."*

Similar emails and conversations have been reported by popular magazines and blogs much to the entertainment of their readers.

On December 11, 2014, The Interview premiered amidst tight security, at a packed house in The Theatre at the Ace Hotel in downtown Los Angeles where Seth Rogen thanked Amy *"for having the balls to make this movie."* Two days later, in a message posted to Pastebin content hosting site, the hackers promised SPE a Christmas gift comprising *"...larger quantities of data. And it will be more interesting. The gift will surely give you much more pleasure and put Sony Pictures into the worst state[120]."*

GOP's messages surfaced on December 16, 2014, warning filmgoers that it planned to stage 9/11-style attack on theaters that played The Interview, and soon five of America's biggest cinema chains decided to drop the film, leading SPE to cancel its Christmas release of the flick in the U.S. On December 18, 2014, former employees whose identity had been exposed, slapped a third class-action lawsuit on SPE, frustrated with the studio's slow response in the matter.

According to many reports, the hackers told SPE in an email on December 19, 2014 that pulling The Interview was a *"very wise decision,"* throwing hints that as long as the film remained canned, away from *"theaters and elsewhere [maybe other channels like video on demand],"* the cyber invasion would cease. Meanwhile, the FBI publicly confirmed that it had enough information to conclude that the North Korean government was responsible for these actions. Bruce

---

120 Kim Zetter; "Sony Hackers Threaten to Release a Huge 'Christmas Gift' of Secrets;" WIRED; Dec. 15, 2014.

Bennett, a Rand expert in Northeast Asian military issues, announced that he had seen The Interview as a favor to Michael Lynton, who happened to be on the Rand board of trustees. He also thought it should be released since the movie wasn't *"going to be good for him [Kim Jong-un]*[121]*"* and his image internally, once the country's privileged classes got around to watching and sharing it. By contrast, California-based threat security firm Norse Corporation, noted for its reporting of Iran's cyberwarfare capabilities, concluded that the SPE hack was in all likelihood the handiwork of a disgruntled ex-employee, probably laid off in May 2014, who was then joined in the plot by a gang of five hackers or pro-privacy hacktivists.

Talking to reporters at his annual year-end press conference, President Obama admitted that SPE as a corporation had certainly suffered significant damage and there were threats against its staff, adding that he thought *"they [SPE] made a mistake [in pulling The Interview] ...[Wish] "they'd...spoken to me first...*[122]*"*

On December 21, 2014, North Korea's rhetoric grew shriller as it insisted the U.S. was behind the making of The Interview. As a result, there was a threat to launch attacks on *"the White House, the Pentagon, and the whole U.S. mainland."* In a 180-degree turn that earned praise from many, including President Obama, SPE confirmed that starting Christmas Eve, it was allowing

---

121 CBS58 Staff; "FBI: North Korea responsible for SONY hack;" Dec. 19, 2014; https://www.cbs58.com/news/fbi-north-korea-responsible-for-sony-hack

122 Samantha Schoenfeld; President says Sony made a mistake canceling release of "The Interview"; Sony CEO disagrees; Dec. 19, 2014; https://fox61.com/2014/12/19/president-says-sony-made-a-mistake-canceling-release-of-the-interview-sony-ceo-disagrees/

The Interview to be released in 200+ cinemas in the U.S., besides making it available on YouTube, GooglePlay, Xbox, seetheinterview.com (Sony's dedicated website) and via video-on-demand. The film's stars like James Franco burst with joy on Twitter: *"VICTORY!!!!!!! The PEOPLE and THE PRESIDENT have spoken!!! SONY to release THE INTERVIEW in theaters..."*

In September 2018, U.S. Department of Justice announced it had issued an arrest warrant in June 2018 for Park Jin Hyok in connection with the hack. Park worked for North Korea's military intelligence and was linked to the Lazarus Group. As previously noted, the Lazarus Group is North Korean-backed cyber espionage group responsible for the theft of $851 million from Bangladesh Bank's Federal Reserve in New York (2016) and the WannaCry Ransomware Menace (2017).

Chapter Eleven

Pulling the Cyber Strings

Several times in the past, Iran has been a victim of cyberattacks, most of which were perpetrated by the U.S. and Israel. Stuxnet, for instance, was a cyber worm that infiltrated Iran's nuclear facility in Natanz in June 2010. Even though the Iranian government claimed that no significant damage was caused by the worm, the country went on to devise a fairly strong defense mechanism, and in offensive cyber operations, it has carried out quite a few successful attacks on other countries since then. Since 2010, the Cyber Defense Command (Gharargah-e- Defa-e Saiberi) is said to be perpetrating cyberattacks on behalf of the Iranian state under the supervision of Iran's Passive Civil Defense Organization, (Sazeman-e Padafand-e Gheyr-e Amel), a specialized unit of the Joint Staff of Iranian Armed Forces.

With time, Iran's cyberwarfare strategy has come of age. According to a 2014 report by the Institute for National Security Studies[123], an Israeli think-tank, *"Iran has become one of the most active players in the international cyber arena."* Moreover, in 2013, a General of the Islamic Revolutionary Guard Corps (IRGC) declared that Iran had become the 4th biggest cyber power among the world's cyber armies.

Like North Korea, Iran uses its substantial cyber army to get around the sanctions imposed on it by the U.S. and Western powers. So far, Western analysts have accused the Iranian government of launching cyberattacks against Israel, the U.S., and Persian Gulf Arab countries.

Recently, Iran's cyberspace activities have been in the spotlight because of the country's involvement in several cyberspace incidents, including an attack on the Saudi Arabian oil company, the theft of internet security permissions, and the hacking of computers at American banks.

Iran's Cyberspace Strategy

There are two fundamental reasons as to why Iran has become an aggressive force in the cyber arena. The first is that Iran has a conscious strategy to keep its citizens under surveillance. The outbreaks that followed the 2009 Iranian presidential elections and those which erupted during the 2011 Arab Spring pro-democracy protests, prompted the Iranian regime to

---

123 "Israeli Think Tank Acknowledges Iran as Major Cyber Power, Iran Claims its 4th Biggest Cyber Army in World;" HaclRead; Oct. 18, 2013; https://www.hackread.com/iran-biggest-cyber-army-israel/

find new ways to use cyber tools to keep tabs on its own citizens in creative ways. The second reason was the cyberattacks made on Iran. In 2012, Iran's Supreme Leader, Ali Khamenei, announced the setting up of a Supreme Cyberspace Council composed of senior government representatives.

The modus operandi of Iran in cyberspace follows two underlying assumptions. The first concerns the development of defensive cyber capabilities that can keep Iran's national security intact and prevent cyberattacks by hostile nations like the U.S. and Israel. The second assumption concerns the development of fierce and offensive capabilities, so the country can combat what it calls *"American superiority"* and control of the global internet infrastructure.

In addition, the Iranian regime wanted to prevent the percolation of Western ideas into the country that could possibly undermine its hold on the state. It's adopted method included the subversion of digital certificate firms so that Iranian hackers could impersonate safe sites and trace social media use of dissidents and make inferences about what they were writing and who was reading their content.

Experts continue to predict that as the face-off between Iran and Western powers over the former developing nuclear program continues to escalate, Iran could launch cyberattacks against some major infrastructures, including financial institutions and power plants on American soil. Iranian officials have stated this openly in their local newspapers. In July 2011, an article in the Iranian newspaper Kayhan, regarded as Khamenei's voice, warned the U.S. to take care of its most vital assets as they risk being brought down by an attack carried out by *"an unknown player somewhere in the world."* Since then, Iranian hackers, who generally have no official affiliation with the establishment, have been consistently involved in cyberattacks, stealing information, causing internet crashes, committing credit card fraud, and more.

Iran has made major investments amounting to more than $1 billion in the acquisition and development of technologies and training of experts that can help advance both offensive and defensive cyber capabilities. In building and operating its cyberspace strategy, Iran focuses on the following components the most:

Training Manpower

Universities like Sharif University of Technology and Amikabir University of Technology offer advanced degrees in computer engineering and mathematics. Amikabir University also has research labs that specialize in data security and secure systems analysis.

Government organizations like the Science Ministry invest astounding sums of money to support and promote computer communications and IT companies. Besides, the Iranian regime also runs hi-tech parks that are engaged in data security research. One of these hi-tech centers, Pardis Technology Park, is so advanced that it is called the Iranian Silicon Valley. The park was established in 2001 by the Presidential Bureau and the Technology Cooperation Office and has since grown at a fast and furious pace to house 400 IT companies today.

Technological Empowerment

The Iranian regime has bought and developed

advanced technological systems that allow the country to monitor information traffic on mobile and computer networks in the country. One of the biggest government-controlled telecom players in Iran, Telecommunications Company of Iran recently, bought high-tech surveillance systems worth $130 million from China's ZTE, capable of tracking information on computer networks, and telephone and cellular lines.

Perhaps the harsh sanctions imposed on Iran for such a long span of time have taught the country many important lessons in empowering itself technologically. Iran is busy developing website filtering and blocking technologies because sanctions prevent the country from buying data filters made by Western countries. One of the best data filters that Iran has developed to date is Spear, developed by Amnafzar. One of its redeeming features is that it can change its filtering strategy continuously, thus making it difficult to circumvent. Using Spear, Iran has reportedly restricted the flow of information into and within the country. An extensive research conducted by OpenNet Initiative, which keeps a close watch on internet filtering, identified Iran as one of the leading nations in website blocking and filtering, alongside countries like China, North Korea, Syria, and Myanmar.

The regime also initiated a project of its own to establish a separate and independent national network – Halal – that is completely isolated from the World Wide Web, to ensure total control over Iranian cyberspace and online content. In addition, Halal makes cyberattacks on Iranian infrastructures much more difficult. Iran has a video channel, Mehr, on the lines of YouTube channel, as well as Padvish, its homegrown antivirus.

Building a Force

The crowning achievement of Iran's cyberspace force is the establishment in 2012 of the Supreme Cyberspace Council, headed by the country's president. It counts among its members senior government representatives and other ministers of science, communications, culture, the chief of police, and the president of the Islamic Propaganda Organization.

One of the leading defensive cyberspace entities is the Center for Information Security, known as MAHER, under the Communications and Information Technologies Ministry. MAHER is responsible for activating response teams in charge of computer security incidents in case of any breach in the country's security network. The center is also mandated with training skilled resources, defending government websites, and developing responses to cyber crises.

According to a 2008 analysis, the IRGC cyberspace warfare program inducted 2,400 professionals on a budget of $76 million. The IRGC is a real pro when it comes to developing infected software by inserting malicious codes into counterfeited computer software and developing a range of capabilities to block Wi-Fi networks and communications. They are also past masters in developing malicious codes (technically viruses and worms) capable of affecting networks and attacking target computers, developing specialized tools for penetrating networks and computers to gather confidential intelligence, and passing it on to remote servers. The program also develops delay mechanisms in order to operate computers by a command from control servers or a predetermined schedule.

In addition to all that, the IRGC is also capable of creating electronic warfare systems that can block radar and communications. With heavy investments by the agency in electronic warfare systems and the existing cyberspace warfare capabilities, Iran is in a perfect position to damage the electronic systems of the U.S., in the event of a military confrontation.

The IRGC and Iranian hackers affiliated with them are always active against domestic and global adversaries of the regime. By outsourcing cyber-attacks, IRGC and the Iranian regime are able to claim deniability for such events. One group of hackers, said to be closely involved with the IRGC and steadfast supporters of the regime, is Ashiyane Digital Security. Aside from planning and executing cyberattacks, Ashiyane offers hackers professional training, including inserting pro-Iranian propaganda into Israeli and Western websites and interrupting and crashing them. They also commit credit frauds, infiltrate databases, and carry out identity thefts.

Besides Ashiyane Digital Security, there's also Iran's Cyber Army that consists of professional hackers who go under fictitious identities and break into Western websites, infiltrate them with pro-Iranian content, take over internet traffic and redirect it, thus harming the websites of the regime's opponents.

Similarly, Basij, another organization that assists the IRGC, has also gained momentum in cyberspace. In 2010, Basij established Basij Cyberspace Council to ripple pro-Iranian propaganda across cyberspace, employing thousands of pro-regime bloggers.

Cyberattacks Attributed to Iran

Among Iran's most infamous and devastating cyberattacks are four that truly shocked the world and made Western powers consider Iran as a major threat in cyberspace. These include:

Attack on Comodo and DigiNotar

In 2011, Iran carried out two attacks on companies that provided SSL (secure sockets layer) permissions. The first of these, in March 2011, targeted Comodo, an American company. Several permissions were stolen, including ones related to internet mail services like Google. However, these permissions were withdrawn before the hackers could make use of them. It turns out that anyone with a stolen authorization for mail.google.com domain can hack users' accounts and steal their Gmail passwords.

The source of the attack was revealed to be linked to Iran based on the IP address. Also, the website where the stolen permissions were checked was located in Iran. The permissions were removed from the web once Comodo realized their internet security had been breached.

The attack on Comodo was a well-planned, indicating it was carried out by a state organization, though it failed to achieve its goal. The intrusion was discovered too soon and was neutralized before the permissions could be used.

However, the same thing did not happen when Iranian hackers breached DigiNotar, a major Dutch SSL permissions provider. DigiNotar's databases were attacked from June through August 2011 with severely unpleasant outcomes referred to as Black Tulip. A total of 531 certifications for website verification were stolen and one of these was used to verify the google.com domain. This allowed the hackers to assume this identity and reroute Gmail servers. DigiNotar, which eventually went bankrupt, had to shut down operations after the attack. All of the stolen permissions were fabricated and then used to penetrate users' email accounts, particularly in Iran. According to an analysis ordered by DigiNotar, the attack penetrated more than 300,000 computers, almost 99 percent of which were Iranian. Experts suggest that Iranian hackers were behind the attack and that it was carried out for internal security purposes or to identify and track down domestic threats to the regime.

Attack on a Group of Financial Institutions in America

According to a formal report issued in the U.S. in September 2012, several American financial institutions were also attacked, such as sites belonging to the Bank of America, Citigroup, and Morgan Chase, as well as some small and medium banking businesses. U.S. authorities believe these intrusions were financed by Iran, not by random hackers, in retaliation for the U.S. sanctions imposed on the country.

Consequently, the Financial Services Information Sharing and Analysis Center issued a notification to all banks in the U.S., alerting them about cyberattacks designed to steal identities via email, Trojan horses, and other malicious tools for registering keystrokes and retrieving user and employee IDs and passwords. Izz ad-Din al-Qassam Cyberspace Fighters claimed responsibility for the attack. The hacker collective announced that the attack on the Bank of America and the NYSE was provoked by a movie that mocked the Prophet Muhammad.

Aramco Attack

In August 2012, almost 30,000 computers at Saudi Arabian oil company, Aramco, were attacked allegedly with help from some insiders who enjoyed high-level access to the machines. This was one of the most devastating cyberattacks ever carried out by a country against any company. Aramco's assets were attacked by Shamoon, a virus that soon spread through the system and destroyed all of the stored information. The saving grace was that the damage was limited to office computers, and operational and control systems were unaffected.

Cybersecurity player Symantec was the first to identify Shamoon in 2012 and according to its official report[124]:

"The Shamoon virus was specially designed to destroy computer systems and IT equipment of an organization, not its control system. The virus was not similar to Stuxnet, the sophisticated cyberwarfare tool that damaged Iran's nuclear program in 2010. The purpose of this attack was not intelligence gathering but to destroy data and computers."

The virus entered the company's systems with the

124 Symantec Official Blog; "Shamoon: Back from the dead and destructive as ever;" Nov. 2016; https://www.symantec.com/connect/blogs/shamoon-back-dead-and-destructive-ever

help of an insider with direct access to the system. The colluder used a USB to deliver the virus to the target systems. The hackers seemed to be affiliated with a political or religious (Islamic) group since they used the image of a burning American flag to obscure the contents of the files in the infected computers. The code of Shamoon's deletion mechanism had the word *"Wiper"* used in it, the same word used in the virus code of Flame that attacked an Iranian oil company. This was a clear indication that the attack was in retaliation for the Flame incident.

The group that claimed responsibility for the attack on Aramco - The Cutting Sword of Justice - confessed that the offensive was an attempt to weaken Saudi Arabia's main source of income, namely, oil. The group declared that the attack was more than successful and was carried out to avenge Saudi Arabia's crimes against Syria and Bahrain.

There have been similar cyberattacks against several other oil and gas companies in the Persian Gulf. Leon Panetta, former U.S. Secretary of Defense, hinted at Iranian involvement in these cybercrimes. Jeffrey Carr, an American cybersecurity expert, raised various allegations that linked Iran to all these cyberattacks. Carr stated that Iran was the only country in the world that had access to the original Wiper code, which formed the basis for the Shamoon virus. According to a report issued by cybersecurity firm Kaspersky, the Wiper code was also used in the attack on the Iranian Energy Ministry in April 2012. Lebanese Shia group Hezbollah's involvement was also suspected in the Aramco attack, and a number of Lebanese employees of Aramco were taken into custody and interrogated.

Infiltration of Indiana Government Computers

In March 2018, Iranian hackers were accused of infiltrating computers of the Indiana state government and the Indiana Department of Education, which affected thousands of college professors and university computers. According to federal law enforcement, the Iran cyber-attack was underway from 2013 until late 2017.

The U.S. is halfway around the world from Iran; even so, hackers working out of Tehran successfully targeted the Indiana state computers located 6,500 miles away. The hacker team was affiliated with the IRGC and allegedly led by Gholamreza Rafatnejad, a private contractor based in Iran. According to U.S. authorities, the team hacked the emails and files of at least 100,000 university professors from around the world, stealing their login credentials, and accessing university databases and college library systems. The U.S. colleges that were infiltrated are among 320 universities around the world that met a similar fate.

The hackers would email professors pretending to be teachers at other schools. They would feign interest in the professors' academic expertise and include fake links to other articles. When the professors went to the replica site, they would type in their login credentials, unknowingly letting Iranian hackers thousands of miles away steal their personal information.

Reports say the victims of Iranian hackers include the U.S. Department of Labor, the United Nations, and the Federal Energy Regulatory Commission. Owing to the audacity demonstrated by carrying out such powerful cyberattacks, Iran is considered a serious threat to America's critical infrastructures. It's obvious that Iran, a victim of some of the most destructive cyberattacks, has learned its lesson and understands the power that lies in developing an offensive tool that can damage the vital infrastructures of hostile nations in a matter of minutes.

Chapter Twelve

The 400 lbs. Man[125]

According to U.S. intelligence, the biggest threat we are facing today is not terrorism, but cybercrime. In fact, by the time you have finished reading this chapter, more than 4,000 new viruses and malware programs will have been released online. That's how fast this threat is growing.

It's difficult to name a country that does not perpetrate

---

125 The 400 Pound Hacker refers to a comment made by Republican presidential nominee Donald Trump during the first 2016 United States Presidential Debate in which he disparagingly suggested the hacker in the Democratic National Committee Email Leak could be a someone (an individual operator) on their bed who weighs 400 pounds.

cybercrimes these days to spy on other countries and cement its political influence. In addition, there's a whole army of individual operators out there that never cease to hack the systems of different organizations for both known and unknown reasons. These individual hackers employ various tricks and tools, sometimes because they can and know how to, and sometimes for the thrill of a new technical adventure. The drivers for their actions are different from nation states and hacker groups with a specific political/financial agenda.

A Tsunami of Cybercrimes

Cybercrimes are growing at an astounding rate. In 2014 alone, an estimated 1 billion data records were compromised worldwide in cyber-attacks, while a whopping 47 percent of Americans had their personal data stolen.

It's not just individuals these ingenious hackers target. The U.S. Department of Defense has to deal with 100,000 cyber-attacks every day and 58 percent of corporate PCs are affected by one or more malware infections. Since stolen data is money lost, cybercrimes cost the global economy up to half a trillion dollars every year. That's the same as the entire world's illegal drugs trade.

Most Wanted Cybercriminals Ever

There's a list of the world's most wanted cybercriminals at the end of this chapter, but there's one notorious cybercriminal who deserves a separate *"recognition."* There was a brief mention of his name and attacks led by him in one of the previous chapters as well. Evgeniy Mikhailovich Bogachev is a Russian hacker who tops the list of the world's most wanted cybercriminals, with the FBI offering a reward of up to $3 million for information leading to his arrest.

This hacking mastermind is known online as *"lucky12345,"* and his scheme involves tricking people into installing the Trojan program *"Game over ZeuS,"* which captures bank details, passwords, and other personal info. It has infected over 1 million computers and earned Bogachev a fortune of $100 million. He's even reported to have installed ransomware in a Massachusetts police station. Ransomware, as discussed in an earlier chapter, is a type of malware that stops users from accessing their files, and demands they pay a ransom in order to regain access. It is unlikely that Bogachev will ever be arrested, since Russia does not extradite accused criminals to other countries.

World's Other Most Notorious Cybercriminals

Now that we are living in a high-tech era, cybercriminals are basically the most dangerous of all conmen and the hardest to catch. Some of the following cyber bandits have been brought to justice, while some names still exist on the most wanted hackers' list.

Nicolae Popescu

Nicolae Popescu is alleged to have posted fraudulent advertisements on internet auction market sites for sale of merchandise. He then negotiated via email with buyers in the U.S. using false identities to send fraudulent invoices with instructions for payment to his bank accounts. The U.S. Department of State's

Transnational Organized Crime Program[126] is offering a reward of up to $1 million for information leading to the arrest of Popescu.

Viet Quoc Nguyen

Viet Quoc Nguyen hacked at least eight email service providers and stole proprietary marketing data comprising over 1 billion email addresses. He then launched spam attacks on tens of millions of them. Nguyen also profited by way of commission on sales for directing internet traffic to websites that promote certain products.

Joshua Samuel Aaron

Between 2007 and 2015, Aaron hacked computer systems of leading U.S. companies to acquire contact details of millions of U.S. customers. He used this information to manipulate prices and volumes of traded shares in numerous publicly traded stocks using deceptive and misleading email campaigns and manipulative prearranged stock trading. Aaron is wanted by both the FBI and the U.S. Secret Service.

Alexsey Belan

Belan invaded the computer networks of three major e-commerce companies in Nevada and California. Allegedly, he stole user data from millions of accounts

---

126 The Transnational Organized Crime Rewards Program was established by Congress in 2013 as a tool to assist the U.S. Government to identify and bring to justice members of significant transnational criminal organizations.

and then negotiated the sale of such data. Belan is also accused of possessing 15 or more unauthorized access devices. The FBI is offering a $100,000 reward for information leading to Belan.

Carlos Enrique Perez Melara

Perez Melara invented a program called *"Lover Spy"* to catch cheating lovers by sending them an electronic greeting that when opened would spontaneously install a spyware program. The spyware collected the person's keystroke logs, passwords, browser history, and incoming and outgoing messages and sent all the collected information periodically back to the person who purchased the service. Melara carries a reward of $50,000 offered by the FBI.

Jonathan James

At 15, this child prodigy hacked into basically everything he could, from the system of the Florida-based Miami Dade School to the U.S. Defense Threat Reduction Agency. He even wormed into NASA systems and ended up stealing $1.7 million worth of software designed to control the physical environment of the International Space Station. Consequently, NASA was forced to shut down its systems for about 3 weeks, which cost them $41,000. In 2000, James was convicted on two counts of juvenile delinquency.

Matthew Bevan and Richard Pryce

The 16-year-old Richard Pryce and his 21-year-old mentor Matthew Bevan committed a series of hacks against government agencies. The duo is responsible for hacking into the systems of NASA, U.S. Air Force, and NATO. They copied battlefield simulations and, not contented with that, hacked into the Korean Atomic Research Institute's database and ended up copying the information onto the U.S Air Force systems. The U.S. was concerned that if North Korea found out, they could accuse the Americans of spying. Providentially, the stolen data turned out to be South Korean.

Edward Majerczyk

In 2014, this serial hacker cracked the iCloud and Gmail accounts of hundreds of celebrities, including actor Jennifer Lawrence, to obtain nudes for his personal use. However, the hack, which has come to be known as *"The Fappening"* or *"Celebgate,"* didn't last long and these nude images found their way onto the internet for everyone to see. It seemed Majerczyk was able to break into iCloud accounts with a simple email address. He was convicted in September 2016.

Gary McKinnon

Gary McKinnon, a British citizen, is considered one of the most dangerous hackers in history after being accused of hacking into 97 U.S. military and intelligence systems for a thirteen-month period, starting in 2002. He deleted important files, and during one of his attacks, he caused 2,000 computers on one network alone to be shut down.

Kevin Mitnick

In the early '90s, Mitnick successfully hacked into almost every big company of the day - Nokia, Motorola, and IBM, and stole their corporate secrets. However, in 1993, after hacking into Pacific Bill telecom, he became the subject of an FBI investigation. Mitnick was on the run for 2-1/2 years. Finally, when he was caught and tried in court in 1995, the jury found him so threatening that for eight months of his total 5-year sentence, he was placed in solitary confinement.

Behzad Mesri

Behzad Mesri, otherwise known as Skote Vahshat, is an Iranian hacker on FBI's most-wanted list responsible for hacking into HBO's systems and stealing unaired episodes of the Game of Thrones TV series, besides hands-on scripts, plot outlines, and other unaired episodes of Ballers, The Deuce, and Curb Your Enthusiasm. He demanded $6 million in bitcoin as ransom money from HBO.

Mohammad Saeed Ajily

Ajily is wanted by the FBI for hacking into a government defense contractor in Vermont, engaged in making software that supports aerodynamics analysis and projectile designs. Ajily is accused of selling the rocket software he stole to Iranian entities, including the military, universities, and government.

This is a relatively small list of cybercriminals, but the full list is almost never-ending. The stakes are getting higher and more dangerous. Perpetrating cybercrimes in the current day and age is a whole different ball game.

How Does Bulletproof Hosting Contribute to Cybercrimes?

Since all these cyber threats such as malware botnets, ransomware are illegal in most countries, they have to be stored some place. Bulletproof hosting is similar to regular hosting except that bulletproof hosting companies are more lenient about what users can store on their servers. They follow the dictum – *"don't ask, don't tell."* This means users are free to store stolen data obtained via data breaches, credit card databases, and corporate espionage. They also host black market websites that promote online gambling, pornography, and sale of illegal items. They also host stolen PayPal accounts and also stolen data stashes and malware storage. These sites ignore requests for takedowns based on copyright violations and any outreach from the law.

Before it was taken down in 2008, McColo, one such bullet web hosting service provider, was responsible for two-thirds of all spam on the internet. Another web hosting service called the Russian Business Network required customers to commit a cybercrime before being allowed to use their service! They were suspected of operating the Storm botnet, which, at its height in September 2007, infected up to 50 million computers worldwide.

In a fascinating detailed article, Brian Krebs[127] described the details of a cybercriminal Yalishanda, whose real name was Aleksandr Volosovyk, and has been labeled as a top-tier bulletproof hosting providers worldwide. As such, Yalishanda facilitated an enormous amount of cybercriminal activity by providing access and infrastructure to cybercrime groups and individuals. Several websites were used by Yalishanda

---

127 Brian Krebs; "Meet the World's Biggest 'Bulletproof' Hoster;" KrebsOnSecurity; Jul. 16, 2019; https://krebsonsecurity.com/2019/07/meet-the-worlds-biggest-bulletproof-hoster/

including mail.ru and abushost.ru. In a talk at the 2017 BlackHat conference, a cyber intelligence firm Intel 471 provided details[128] about Yalishanda's operations and many hosting sites tied to his infrastructure with ties to banking trojans and ransomware operations.

Why Is It Difficult to Catch Cybercriminals?

Around 70 percent of the cybercrime crisscrosses national borders, which can make it difficult to catch perpetrators. What is illegal in one country might not be considered illegal or may be tolerated in another. According to a UN report, [129]controlling or sending spam was not a criminal offense in 63 percent of countries, including India, Russia, and Brazil. It doesn't matter that the spam can carry a malicious code that could potentially track a user, steal data, or install malware.

Despite being the biggest facilitator of illegal file sharing on this planet, The Pirate Bay continues to operate after more than a decade online. How is that even possible? In 2006, after its offices were raided and servers taken down, the torrent indexing platform was back in business in three days' time. It turns out, the site is enabled by a widespread network of servers, so shutting down one doesn't make a difference to its functioning. In 2007, The Pirate Bay attempted but failed to buy the self-declared tiny sovereign state of Sealand in the North Sea in order to create their own country with no copyright laws. To put themselves beyond the reach of police raids, The Pirate Bay moved their operations to the cloud. Cloud computing brings huge benefits, but it

---

128 RBN Reloaded - Amplifying Signals from the Underground
https://www.youtube.com/watch?v=PGTTRN6Vs-Y
129 United Nations Office on Drugs and Crime; Comprehensive Study on Cybercrime; Feb. 2013.

has also opened doors for cybercriminals to carry out attacks in ways that were not possible before. Today, The Pirate Bay servers run on over 20 virtual machines and the providers don't even know they are hosting this torrenting website.

Unrestricted Freedom

Online anonymity offered by bulletproof web hosting services is used by journalists and whistleblowing sites like WikiLeaks to avoid state censorship. The freedom can be exploited by terror networks and individual agents of chaos. In a U.S. government hearing, it was disclosed that two of the three biggest chatrooms used by ISIS, the jihadist militant group, were shielded by CloudFlare, a bulletproof web hosting service.

According to the hacktivist group Anonymous, ISIS' cybercriminals use the service to protect up to 40 terrorist websites devoted to propaganda, discussion, and terror training. They have also reportedly leaked contact information of the head leaders of the CIA, FBI, and NSA.

Dark Web and Cybercrimes

The untraceable anonymity of the dark web, a portion of the internet that is inaccessible to normal search engines, makes it a perfect setting for cybercriminals looking to make serious money. An estimated 9 percent of all listings on the dark web are to do with fraud. Stolen card details sell for as little as $5, while login details for a $20,000 bank account are peddled for, say, $1,200. By the way, those are just some of the petty hacks, but operators are increasingly using the dark web for more serious activities (e.g., sale of drugs and firearms, hiring hackers and hitmen). Illegal drugs trade reportedly accounts for more than 15 percent of all dark web sites. One such site, The Silk Road, netted $80 million in commission from a whopping $1.2 billion of sales for owner Ross Ulbricht before being shut down in 2013.

Dawn of a New Era of Cybercrime

The only thing hacking enthusiasts need today to carry out a cyber-attack is a PC. They can perpetuate a cyber war while sitting in their homes. The biggest example of individual operators waging a cyber war is Carbanak[130]. Chances are most people have not heard of Carbanak, but it's actually responsible for the biggest cyber heist in history, stealing $1 billion from over 100 financial institutions worldwide. The hackers in Russia, Ukraine, and China did it all between 2013 and 2015 while still glued to their keyboards.

Emails infected with Carbanak malware allowed individual hackers in different parts of the world to record what happened on the screens of banking staff. After months of studying behavior, they would transfer money to their own accounts or order ATMs to give out cash at predetermined times. In a single raid, the hackers could steal up to $10 million.

In this instant the "400-lb man" turned out to be three Ukrainian nationals – Dmytro Fedorov, aka

---

130 One of the more detailed descriptions of the Carbanak APT is offered by Kaspersky Labs who supported the effort to investigate the theft of nearly $1bn from 100 financial institutions worldwide. The theft mostly came by remotely controlling ATM's and having them spit out cash at predetermined hours and day. See, "Carbanak APT: The Great Bank Robbery;" V2.1; Feb. 2015; Kasperksy Lab.

"Hotdima;" Fedir Hladyr, aka "Das;" and Andrii Kopakov, aka "Santisimo." Copies of their indictment were published by the US Department of Justice[131]

---

131   https://www.justice.gov/opa/pr/three-members-notorious-international-cybercrime-group-fin7-custody-role-attacking-over-100

SECTION IV:

Technological Connectedness

Chapter 13: How IoT (The Internet of Things) Is Making It Harder for Cybersecurity

Case Study Seven: Chris Roberts – "Plane Hacker"

Chapter Thirteen

How IoT (The Internet of Things) Is Making It Harder for Cybersecurity

In April 2015, Chris Roberts, a U.S. hacker, was detained by the FBI after officials saw his Twitter posts about hacking into the plane he was traveling on. According to extensive investigation by the FBI, Roberts has the ability to take over flight controls by hacking into the inflight entertainment (IFE) system.

Chris Roberts, founder of Denver-based One World Labs, a security intelligence firm, is widely considered as an expert on counter-threat cybersecurity. Roberts claimed in one of his interviews with FBI agents in February 2015 that he managed to hack into the IFE systems of Airbus and Boeing aircraft, midflight, not once but 15 to 20 times between 2011 and 2014. As per FBI's search warrant application, in one of his hacking attempts, Roberts physically accessed the IFE system through the Seat Electronic Box (SEB) installed under the passenger seat in front of him. Robert hacked the IFE system using his laptop and a Cat6 Ethernet cable with a modified connector. He then overrode the code on the plane's thrust management computer and took control of one of the plane's engines for a moment. He issued a *"CLB"* (climb) command that made the plane move sideways. Roberts told FBI that on one occasion he hacked into airplane networks and could even monitor air traffic from the cockpit system. In one of his tweets, Roberts also went on to say, *"Over the last 5 years my only interest has been to improve aircraft security."*

A biography of Roberts, shared by One World Labs, lavishes praise on his hacking wizardry:

> *"Regarded as one of the world's foremost experts on counter threat intelligence within the cybersecurity industry, Roberts constructs and directs One World Labs' comprehensive portfolio of cyber defense services designed to improve the physical and digital security posture of both its enterprise and government clients. Roberts understands enterprise security requirements, having served as both an in-house security expert and consultant on IT security, engineering, and architecture/design operations for scores of Fortune 500 companies across the finance, retail, energy and services sectors. Further, he regularly engages with various government agencies on critical security issues of national importance."*[132]

132 M. Justin, 2015, Hacker Chris Roberts told FBI he took control of United plane, FBI Claims, https://www.washintonpostcom/news/morning-mix/wp/2015/05/18/hacher-chris-roberts-told-fbi-he-tood-control-of-united-plane-fbi-claims/?noredirect=on&utm_term=.c4bbaa902906

FBI believes Roberts knew the weaknesses in three types of Boeing aircraft and one Airbus model. This awareness of vulnerabilities made it easier for him to hack into IFE systems made by Panasonic and Thales. Roberts has given several media interviews in which he has discussed airline system vulnerabilities at length. Talking to Fox News, he said, *"Quite simply put, we can theorize on how to turn the engines off at 35,000 ft and not have any of those damn flashing lights go off in the cockpit."*

Roberts' intention behind his hacking attempts might have been to surface the deficiencies in the systems aboard Boeing and Airbus aircraft, but there are other hackers who might end up causing severe damage and loss by carrying out similar hacking attempts. Realizing the imminent threat, GAO was asked to conduct a study to evaluate the cybersecurity efforts by the U.S. Federal Aviation Administration (FAA) responsible for supervising the national airspace system, which comprises air traffic control (ATC) systems, facilities, procedures, aircraft, and the people who operate them.

In its study, GAO highlighted three areas in which the FAA faced cybersecurity challenges:

- Protection of Air Traffic Control (ATC) information systems

- Safety of aircraft avionics used to operate and guide aircraft

- Lack of clarity with regard to the cybersecurity roles and responsibilities of multiple FAA offices

FAA has taken drastic measures to protect its ATC systems from cyber threats. However, still there are major security control weaknesses that pose a threat to the agency's ability to ensure safe operation of the national airspace system. The biggest risk is that contemporary aircraft are increasingly plugged into the Internet. According to the GAO: *"This interconnectedness can potentially provide unauthorized remote access to aircraft avionics systems."* The same interconnectedness allowed Roberts to hack into Airbus and Boeing aircraft IFE systems.

With the advent of the Internet of Things (IoT), the landscape of cyber-based threats has become more dangerous than it ever was. It's not just the aircraft, even weapons, homes, cars, and entire industries are hardwired to the internet, which puts common people at risk.

What IoT Means and How It Works?

IoT is everywhere. It's in the air conditioners that people can control with their smartphones and in smart cars that provide the shortest route. IoT is in smartwatches that track the user's daily activities. Simply put, IoT is a giant network with connected devices that gather and share data about how they are used and the environment in which they are operated. Data is emitted from various sensors embedded in every physical device, be it a smartphone, vehicle, barcode sensor, or traffic light, or maybe an electrical appliance. In sum, almost everything out there!

IoT provides all these devices a common platform to dump their data and a common language to *"talk"* to each other. The IoT platform integrates the collected data from various devices, and after performing further analysis on the data, it extracts valuable insights. These are then shared with other devices to improve user experience and efficiencies.

Industrial IoT

In air conditioner manufacturing, both the manufacturing machine and the conveyor belt have sensors attached. They continuously send data on the machine's health and production specifics to the manufacturer to help diagnose machinery defects well in advance. A barcode is attached to each product before it leaves the belt, and this contains product descriptors like product code, manufacturer details, and special instructions. The manufacturer uses the data to identify where the product was distributed and track the retailer's inventory; hence, the manufacturer can make the product running out of stock, available just in time. Moreover, these products are packed and parceled to different retailers. Each retailer has a barcode reader to track the products coming from different producers, manage inventory, check special instructions, and much more. The compressor of the air conditioner has an embedded sensor that emits data regarding its health and temperature, and this is analyzed continuously to enable the customer care to contact the customer for maintenance even before the air conditioner can break down.

By 2020, it is predicted that 92 percent of manufacturing organizations would have adopted IoT with a view to improve product quality and workflow efficiency. Further into the future, IoT has the potential to boost global productivity by up to 25 percent by 2025, which could translate to an economic value of $11 trillion. Currently, thousands of IoT sensors have been deployed in manufacturing environments to measure temperature gauges and collect valuable data from the individual components on the conveyor belt. Connecting data from these devices improves business efficiency and fosters innovation.

In the industrial sector, IoT combines the capabilities of analytics, cognitive computing, and the cloud-hosted IBM Watson Internet of Things service to drive operational efficiency across the factory value chain mainly in three ways:

- It helps industrial plants get 100 percent efficiency out of their equipment by identifying and solving issues before they can cause delays.

- It makes operations more cognitive, so plants can produce maximum quality and yield from raw materials and manufactured components.

- It helps plant managers better manage resources in order to improve workers' expertise and provide a safe working environment.

For instance, IoT allows the plant manager for an aircraft manufacturer to identify problems with the equipment's health and performance as well as prescribe maintenance procedures. This way, the plant manager can avoid equipment failure and downtime. IoT ensures the aircraft components are meeting quality standards along the production line. With the help of quality analytics tools, the plant manager can identify variability in the manufacturing process in real time. This results in producing faultless components and saving time and money.

The cognitive IoT platform includes worker safety technology that monitors aspects like exposure to extreme heat or toxic gas, open flames, and dangerous machinery. People who work in factories have sensors in their helmets and wristbands to provide real-time alerts on working conditions, and preventive measures are activated if physical well-being is compromised. Sensors installed in an aircraft continue to generate data over the lifetime of the plane, data that designers and engineers can use to make improvements and updates to each part in the future.

The Connected Home

It's not just industries, homes and offices are also becoming more and more intelligent and automated, thanks to IoT. This has led to the rise of what people call a "smart home" – a home that rides on internet-connectivity to enable homeowners to take control of their appliances and utilities, technically from anywhere around the world, by using their smartphone, tablet, or computer.

Lights in homes can be turned on or off as the sun goes up and down instead of the same time every day. If there has been unexpected snow, people can start the engines of their cars from their smartphones and turn the heating on. They can operate the stereo volume in their house from afar and see how warm or cold it is in their house. If they want, they can turn on an extra heating element directly from their smartphones, so when they return, their house is warm.

Homeowners can also limit the use of their electrical gadgets from their smartphones, regardless of where they are on this planet. They can even lock and unlock the doors of their house from any corner of the world. Remote controlled sprinklers, robot lawnmowers, video doorbells, and home assistants, like Amazon's Echo, are some of the many IoT devices that make homes "smart."

The Connected City

Internet-connected devices cannot only make an ordinary home smart, they can connect a society and also make a city smart. Yingtan is a shining example of how smart a small city can be. This 3,560 sq. km city in China with 1.3 million people is the site of Asia's largest copper production. As an enthusiastic advocate of the smart city concept in China, Yingtan is spearheading the development of mobile IoT. It is the first city in the world to deploy narrow band IoT (NB-IoT) across its entire administrative region. A total of 962 NB-IoT-based stations now dot Yingtan's landscape.

The network availability rate in Yingtan has reached an impressive 95 percent, the first to reach this level within the nation. The NB-IoT network quality can meet the requirements of diverse industries in various application scenarios, such as monitoring of underground pipelines and parking lots, and forest fire prevention.

Currently, a total of 41 IoT enterprises have set up shops in Yingtan. Together, they have launched more than 30 types of IoT products, ranging from enterprise to personal, accounting for 75 percent of the world's total. Yingtan serves as a test bed for trial applications of 15 usage scenarios, involving over 48,000 connected terminals. Smart Yingtan features intelligent interconnection and will ultimately bring win-win results for all parties involved.

With smart appliances, smart cars, smart homes, and smart cities, IoT is redefining people's lifestyle and transforming the way they interact with technologies. The future of IoT is huge. According to Business Insider Intelligence[133], 24 billion IoT devices will be installed by 2020. ITC predicts that IoT revenue will reach around $357 billion in 2019, resulting in a lot of job opportunities in the IT industry.

IoT as a Threat to Cybersecurity

Smart cars, smart homes, and smart cities let people live a cozy life, but IoT also brings some dark and scary thoughts around a whole new level of cyber-based risks. Smart homes and buildings are evolving into what we call complex IoT environments (CIEs). A CIE consists of at least ten IoT devices that are functionally chained to one another and integrated into an environment that uses an IoT automation platform. This complexity works to make life fast, smart, and easy but also lays these environments open to various cyberattacks.

Trend Micro Research[134] described several examples in Europe and United States of smart homes, buildings, and other structures to note cyber threats which could potentially endanger the facility. In their example of how CIEs work, a smart alarm function was set up, which would be triggered when an intruder was detected in a particular home. This configuration linked the speaker, lights, blinds, locks, and other IoT devices to

---

133   https://www.businessinsider.com/there-will-be-34-billion-iot-devices-installed-on-earth-by-2020-2016-5

134 Cybersecurity Risks in Complex IoT Environments: Threats to Smart Homes, Buildings and Other Structures; Trend Micro Research, 2019.

activate simultaneously, since they are all functionally *"chained"* by means of a code or logic in order to expose the intruder.

The smart alarm connected to the CIE would check if all doors and windows were closed and send an SMS notification to the house owner's phone. A single change in the code tampered the entire environment. Even though the door was open, the notification received by the owner said all doors were closed. So, if a hacker is able to make a similar change in the code, he can get the door locks to open when motion is detected by the backdoor camera. That's how fragile cybersecurity is with IoT.

Poor configuration can also make smart environments vulnerable to threats. Take for example a smart speaker quite popular in many homes. If a homeowner turns on the alarm system through the smart speaker before leaving the house, it can be turned off by sending a text-to-speech command to the speaker, making it very convenient for intruders to barge into a house or office.

Similarly, a hacker can intercept the radio signals sent by, say, smart light bulbs. By identifying the frequency used, a hacker can capture the signals and open the garage door of a smart home. Using the same tactic, a hacker can jam an entire building by overloading the system with repeated radio signal transmissions.

These simple tactics enable attackers to breach security in CIE, which puts smart homes, smart buildings, smart vehicles, and smart industrial settings at significant risk.

Many automotive researchers believe that hackers can actually take control of vehicles wirelessly. A hacker can take control of a car's brakes, door locks, and its computerized dashboard displays by gaining access to the onboard computer through in-vehicle safety and security systems like GM's OnStar and Ford's Sync. This sort of hacking does not even require any physical access to a car's onboard diagnostics port. All hackers need is a car with a Bluetooth system, which would allow them to execute a code to steal the control of the car from its owner's hands. Another way to hack into a car is through its media player. A Toyota Prius was reportedly hacked, and its computerized braking systems hijacked using some of these tactics in 2013.

Researchers have found that professional hackers can easily break into the safety system that automatically dials *"911"* in the event of a serious crash. They can take over the equipment by breaking through its authentication system.

Hacking duo Charlie Miller and Chris Valasek spent a year or two developing software that could wirelessly sabotage a 2014 Jeep Cherokee without even attaching any device to it. The software was capable of remotely hacking more than 100 models of SUVs over the internet via a cellular connection to the in-car entertainment system. They hacker could do something as trivial as turning on the fan or AC, or take control of the steering wheel, its transmission or brakes. According to Tadayoshi Kohno, an assistant professor of computer science at the University of California, San Diego, *"It's surprising to find that the attack surface is so broad*[135]*."* This means there are numerous ways to breach a car's security and take control of its computer systems.

---

135 Craig Timberg; "Hacks on the highway;" The Washington Post; July 22, 2015.

Researchers have proved that professional hackers can, say, search for the desired models of cars, find out their locations, and unlock them, all of this without any forced entry. On top of all that, IoT has made it easier for hackers to perform malicious surveillance by forcing a vehicle to send out its GPS location at regular intervals.

There's no denying that cars are turning into computers on wheels and airplanes will become flying data centers over time. There are reasonable security controls in place, but still there's a long way to go, especially when it comes to IoT devices that are capable of aiding professional hackers to perpetrate a hack and put human lives in grave danger.

Case Study Seven

Chris Roberts – *"Plane Hacker"*

On April 15, 2015, the Federal Bureau of Investigation (FBI) was advised by a senior manager at United Airlines' Cyber Security Intelligence Department about a few messages from and to the Twitter account Sidragon1 of the passenger in seat 3A on flight #1474 (tail no.3260) from Denver to Chicago on April 15, 2015:

@Sidragon1: "Find myself on a 737/800, lest see Box-IFE-ICE SATCOM? Shall we start playing with EICAS messages? 'PASS OXYGEN ON' Anyone? :)."

@RafalLos: "...aaaaand you're in jail. :-)."

@Sidragon1: "There is a distinct possibility that

the course of action laid out above would land me in an orange suite [sic] rather quickly :)."

The United Airlines representative decoded the usage *"PASS OXYGEN ON"* as a possible reference to the passenger oxygen masks on board while ICE was probably short for in-flight communications equipment or integrated communications equipment. *"SATCOM"* mentioned in the tweet was the satellite communications system installed on certain types of aircraft. A senior manager with the United Airlines' Cyber Security Intelligence Department advised the FBI that EICAS refers to the Engine Indication Crew Alerting System. EICAS provides pilots with critical information about airplane engines. EICAS also warns the crew about system faults via red warning messages/amber caution messages and supports remedial measures.

A United Airlines senior manager informed FBI that flight #1474 carrying the said passenger was equipped with a Thales IFE system with seatback monitors. Two seat electronic boxes (SEBs) were installed in each row on either side of the airplane aisle. After arriving in Chicago on April 15, 2015, the passenger changed to United Airlines flight #3642, which was not equipped with an IFE system, and continued up to Syracuse. Meanwhile, the airline with tail number 3260 flew from Chicago to Philadelphia International Airport (this time with flight no. 1607) and arrived at Gate D13 on April 15, 2015. An FBI special agent examined the SEBs in the airline's first-class cabin and noticed that the SEB under seat 2A was damaged, its outer cover open nearly ½ inch with the retaining screw exposed! The SEB under 3A also showed signs of tampering. Shortly after flight #3642 touched down at Syracuse, two FBI special agents – one of whom was Mark Hurley – and two local police officers got on the plane, and first walked past the passenger at his seat, before turning around to face him. At this, the passenger enquired: *"So should I get my bags now?"* to which he got the response – *"Yes, please, Mr. Roberts."*

Security Tinkerer

If his LinkedIn profile (sidragon1) is any indication, Chris Roberts, 48, is a *"security tinkerer"* and the keywords that describe the nature of his engagements over the years include tech, IT, information security, safety, cyber stuff, and research. At 6-foot-3, all-dressed in kilt (though he cautions *"if you call my kilt a skirt, I will hollow out your head with a spork and replace it with the guts of a ZX80 [home computer]"* trademark ski cap, glasses, and turquoise goatee, Roberts claims to be *"comfortable leaping over fences, training teams, waving hands on stage, talking with boards and generally provoking folks into thinking about safety and security in slightly different ways, hopefully to effect change."*

At 15, (around 1987) Roberts, a British citizen, hacked into his dad's bank account and siphoned its contents into his account. His parents had separated, and the teen was apparently upset with his dad. The following day, the budding hacker was in for a rude surprise as two British policemen turned up at his doorstep and requested him to accompany them to the station. Since the incident looked like a family matter by the standards of that age, both the police and the bank gave it a quiet burial.

A little later, the incurable maverick hacked into his employer's HR database only to discover, much to his chagrin, that he was being paid less than some people he had trained. Roberts didn't manage to get a hike but got fired after he confronted the boss rather tactlessly with this clinching evidence. Having dropped out of Oxford University computer science program, he dabbled in cryptography. Roberts worked in the IT departments of several companies doing *"legit"* work through the 1990s – though his LinkedIn profile captures only his work career since 2002. Outside of work, he had a lot of fun digging through software on his computer, delving into the system's dark secrets.

Between 2002 and December 2009, Roberts worked for a clutch of organizations, namely, Limited Brands, Sports Authority, Webroot, Coalfire Systems, and CCi5, spanning domains like security infrastructure and engineering, cybersecurity, threat intelligence, dark net research, cryptography, deception technologies, and cyber risk management and compliance. In 2009, Roberts co-founded Denver-based IT forensics firm Cyopsis with ex-FBI agent Kevin Knierim. Roberts served as its managing director and lead IT investigator until September 2010, when he decided to strike out on his own since digital forensics involved working with lawyers (he wanted to do less of that).

Aircraft Hacking

Sometime in 2009, Roberts turned his attention to aviation security after perusing aircraft flight manuals and electrical wiring diagrams available in the public domain. He and his colleague poured over the schematics of inflight entertainment systems and concluded that, at least in certain airplanes, these were linked to passenger satellite phone networks, connecting further to some cabin control systems and onward to the plane avionics. Given such interconnectedness, the two researchers conjectured there might be security flaws that a threat actor with malicious intent might be able to exploit with grave consequences.

In January 2010, Roberts founded One World Labs (OWL) reportedly with three employees, and a handful of contractors and temps. OWL's vice president for business relationships Jim Holdridge moved in from a credit card payment provider that Roberts had consulted with previously. In April 2011, at Thotcon, a non-profit, non-commercial hacking conference in Chicago, Roberts and OWL staffer Jesse Diekman presented *"Planes, Trains and Automobiles,"* which ran more or less along the same lines as Roberts' earlier presentation at the BSides security conference. Essentially, the duo underscored the idea that the operating systems of almost all things with engines – mass transit, boats, locomotives, tanks, long-haul passenger aircraft, and large industrial tractors – could be hacked. These machines could be tampered with by rewriting the configuration file of various programs or simply inserting codes in order to manipulate the system or influencing the library (of precompiled routines) used by a program.

On FBI's Radar

In February 2015, an FBI special agent quizzed Roberts in Denver to ferret out facts about security vulnerabilities in airplane IFE systems, and Roberts reportedly shared information on vulnerabilities he had come across in the IFE systems on Boeing 737-800, 737-900, 757-200, and Airbus A-320 aircraft, so these could be patched in a timely manner. The maverick hacker gave the FBI a blow-by-blow account of the methods, tools, and tactics he employed. Once on board the aircraft, he would move the cover of the SEB under the seat in front of him rapidly up, down, sideways and also press it firmly until it came off. While in flight, he would use a Cat6 Ethernet cable with a modified connector to hook his laptop to the SEB and then infiltrate the IFE system using default IDs and passwords, before connecting to other critical systems, thereby putting at risk innocent peoples' lives. Roberts dropped another bombshell; between 2011 and mid-2014, he had infiltrated IFE systems nearly 15-20 times while in flight on airplanes fitted out with either Thales or Panasonic IFE systems and video screens installed on the back of passenger seats.

The FBI agent returned a few weeks later in March 2015 for a more detailed discussion that lasted a couple more hours. This time Roberts' interlocutor wanted to know precisely what Roberts had done during these flights and to what extent aircraft systems could be compromised by malicious intruders. Roberts responded that he and his colleague had sniffed data packets moving along the network data traffic on more than a dozen flights after plugging into IFE networks. On two occasions, on February 13 and February 23, 2015, FBI special agents in Denver reportedly informed Roberts that accessing airplane networks without authorization represented a violation of federal statute and that he might face legal proceedings for obtaining access to airplane networks or scanning airplane networks. Roberts acknowledged the FBI advisory, saying that he understood he should not access airplane networks.

The tweet Roberts sent out from his MacBook Pro on April 15, 2015, while in flight on United Airlines flight #1474 (tail no.3260) from Denver to Chicago, was meant to be a sarcastic joke from his standpoint. It is the height of irony that Roberts was flying into Syracuse to talk to an audience comprising law enforcement but already FBI special agents were lying in wait for the free-spirited security expert. His entire hacking gear, comprising iPad, MacBook Pro, hard drives, flash drives, and Bluetooth adapters, was seized on arrival on the basis of a pending warrant.

The hacking kit that was impounded looked much like standard fare used by almost all security researchers engaged in penetration testing. The affidavit filed by Special Agent Mark Hurley on April 17, 2015, before the U.S. District Court of New York explains why the FBI decided to seize Roberts' equipment based on the following pieces of evidence: (1) the SEB under seat 2A and seat 3A, where Robert sat, on board the Denver-Chicago flight on April 15, 2015, showed signs of tampering; (2) Roberts' tweets during the flight suggested he was about to access the plane's IFE; (3) In his conversations with FBI agents on February 13 and March 5, 2015, he had claimed that using special equipment in his possession, he had infiltrated airplane IFE systems and taken control of other systems on the aircraft network. Taking all of these into account, FBI agents and technical specialists believed that[136]:

"...he [Roberts] may have just done that [hacking the IFE systems] again or attempted to do so [on the Denver-Chicago flight on April 15, 2015] using the equipment then in his possession... we believed that Roberts had the

---

136 "Security expert allegedly told FBI he hacked & steered airliner mid-flight;" RT News; May 17, 2015.

ability and the willingness to use the equipment then with him to access or attempt to access the IFE and possibly the flight control systems on any aircraft equipped with an IFE system and that it would endanger public safety to allow him to leave the Syracuse airport that evening with that equipment. Accordingly, we confiscated the above-referenced equipment at that time."

Roberts took a photo of the impounded devices and later tweeted it from his Sidragon1 account along with the caption: *"Bye-bye electronics, all encrypted... and all now in custody/seized."* He also put out a tweet indicating that he had not received a warrant from the FBI nor had his equipment been returned by them.

During a four-hour interrogation, which Roberts later described as a *"testy, but polite,"* the security wiz told the FBI that after infiltrating the flight's network, he apparently used Vortex software, typically used in video games and physical simulation, to monitor traffic from the cockpit system. He employed Kali Linux, an industry-standard version of the Linux operating system used by ethical hackers to uncover security vulnerabilities, to perform testing of the IFE system. Roberts also told the FBI that he used VBox software to create several virtual machines (secondary operating systems) on his laptop and run them out of it. This virtual environment he had kitted up on his laptop mimicked the airplane network in every detail and he set to work infiltrating this network.

Roberts claimed he overwrote (replaced) code on the plane's thrust management computer responsible for detecting engine parameters and controlling thrust produced by the engine. Not content with just that, during one of the flights – though the FBI affidavit makes no mention of exactly which flight – he went ahead and took control of the computer and issued the *"climb command"* for increasing altitude to one of the airplane engines, causing the plane to move sideways, a dangerously crazy maneuver if true! His interlocutors accused Roberts of tampering with systems on the United flight, but Roberts insisted that he did not compromise the airplane network on United Airlines' Denver-Chicago flight though the thumb drive in his possession contained virtual machines and malware capable of infiltrating networks and his MacBook Pro had been powered on this flight. Besides, he willingly shared with the FBI wiring schema from his MacBook for various aircraft models. The FBI requested Roberts to unlock his laptop and share the password with them, so they could decrypt the hard drive and do a forensic analysis of it to recover deleted and inaccessible files but Roberts summarily turned down the request claiming there was proprietary information stored away on the machine and demanded to see the FBI agents' search warrant.

In May 2015, after the FBI affidavit entered the public domain, talking to Wired magazine, Roberts voiced his concerns that contents of his conversations with the federal agency held behind closed doors had gone public. In some ways, the security expert seemed to be back-pedaling from his earlier claims; he said he hadn't even got as far as connecting his laptop to the SEB on the Denver-Chicago flight. "Nope I did not. That I'm happy to say and I'll stand from the top of the tallest tower and yell that one," he said, adding:[137]

---

137 Ms. Smith; "FBI: Security researcher admitted to hacking planes 15 to 20 times while in-flight;" May 17, 2015; CSO Magazine.

"Those [SEBs] boxes are underneath the seats. How many people shove luggage and all sorts of things under there?... I'd be interested if they looked at the boxes under all the other seats and if they looked like they had been tampered. How many of them are broken and cracked or have scuff marks? How many of those do the airlines replace because people shove things under there?"

On April 18, 2015, Roberts was stopped by United Airlines' security personnel at the boarding gate as he attempted to board one of their flights from Colorado to San Francisco, where the researcher was scheduled to speak at a major security conference. United's spokesperson Rahsaan Johnson told Associated Press that, in the light of Roberts' claims regarding manipulating aircraft systems, *"we've decided it's in the best interest of our customers and crew members that he not be allowed to fly."* Pressed by the media about the nature of threat Roberts posed if United's systems couldn't be compromised, the spokesperson said: *"Mr. Roberts has made comments about having tampered with aircraft equipment...[which] were a violation of United policy and something customers and crews shouldn't have to deal with."* Roberts' lawyer protested that the airline hadn't given his client any detailed explanation why he wasn't allowed on the plane but had instead said they would be sending Roberts a letter stating why they wouldn't let him fly on their aircraft. However, the airline, for its part, said it had informed Roberts several hours before his flight that he couldn't fly. The unrelenting Roberts took an alternative flight on Southwest Airlines to San Francisco and lectured at the RSA Conference about computer security loopholes.

NASA – Hacked?

A video surfaced online in early 2015 showing Roberts bragging to an audience at the GrrCON2012 hacker convention about how eight or nine years earlier he had hacked into NASA's system and fiddled with the federal agency's communication controls to change the temperature on board the International Space Station. Roberts claimed he had also considered taking Curiosity Rover – NASA's car-sized rover, which landed on the surface of Mars in August 2012 – *"for a spin"* after infiltrating it but ultimately, he and his buddies had dropped the plan. The intrepid hacker also claimed that while on board a Boeing 737 jet, he had breached its on-board firewall!

Financial Problems at OWL

Regardless of whether federal authorities have a case or not against Roberts, it's hard to miss some of the collateral effect the incident might have had on his company OWL, which he quit in September 2015 though he still held a majority shareholding. A month later, The *Wall Street Journal* reported that the information security business had filed for bankruptcy, amidst mounting debts to the tune of $720,000. Roberts told Wired magazine that OWL's investors had decided to pull out their money, and as a result, nearly half of its staff, nearly a dozen people, had to be laid off. Roberts said his legal situation *"was probably the final straw"* leading to his investor's decision, though there were other factors as well.

A Couple of Unanswered Questions

Chris Roberts hasn't been charged with any crime, but questions have been rife among security researchers about how ethical and responsible were the methods he adopted in order to draw the world's attention to vulnerabilities in airline software that cybercriminals could possibly exploit to endanger passenger safety. That a security expert of some stature should tamper or attempt to manipulate a plane's network during a flight was quite shocking for many peers in security industry. *"I find it really hard to believe but if that is the case he deserves going to jail,"* wrote Jaime Blasco, director of AlienVault Labs (now *"AT&T Cybersecurity"*), in a tweet. Yahoo's chief of information security, Alex Stamos tweeted, *"You cannot promote the (true) idea that security research benefits humanity while defending research that endangered hundreds of innocents."*

The excitement of hacking got Roberts all fired up and, at some point, he seems to have meandered into the uncharted territory of cheerful, devil-may-care, unauthorized, and unethical cyber intrusion into highly sensitive computer networks. Neither the bohemian cyber specialist nor the FBI has definitive answers to some questions:

- Why didn't Roberts go straight to the FBI back in 2011, when he started tossing around these ideas about hacking operating systems of moving objects (cars, tractors, planes), convince them about the vulnerabilities, and get them to buy in his remedial proposal, if any?

- Conversely why didn't the FBI approach Roberts around the same time?

- Did the FBI turn a deaf ear to Robert's ideas, probably dismissing it as crazy and nerdish bluster?

232

Postscript

After exiting OWL in September 2015, Chris Roberts worked for Sentinel Global, Acalvio Technologies, and LARES Consulting before joining his current employer Attivo Networks in June 2018. As chief security strategist at Attivo, based in San Francisco Bay Area, Roberts' responsibilities include developing and implementing risk reduction strategies. He is a much sought-after speaker at industry conferences and has been regularly featured in the media.

SECTION V:

Future Considerations

Chapter 14: Policies and Preventions

Chapter Fourteen

Policies, Preventions, And A Possible International Cyber Regime

In this chapter, I will explore policy and legal options, which exist today, or which should, be enacted to reduce and control cyber incidents and provide mechanisms to mitigate risks from such incidents. The discussion of policy alternatives is complex as it crosses international boundaries. It requires that harmonized national laws, bilateral and multilateral arrangements must be in place for an effective system which can provide guardrails of control, deterrence, and punishment.

In order to deter or discourage an action or pursuit of action, society has enacted laws and a legal system for the execution of those laws. The enforcement of law is limited to the territory of the State or Nation in which it is enacted. An act which may be a crime in one nation may not be in another nation. Herein lies a rather curious dilemma for cyber actions in that most such acts lie in the transnational space[138].

Consider a cyber perpetrator using various cyber tools (servers, software, internet connectivity) in the pursuit of a cyber intrusion (or a cyber victim). Each of these components may be located in one or more countries. For example, The CSIS reported[139] that in December 2019, a suspected Vietnamese State-sponsored hacking group attacked BMW and Hyundai networks. At first glance, this incident involves the nations of Vietnam, Germany, and S. Korea.

More details of the incident reveal that the group associated with the attack is APT32 or "Ocean Lotus" and it used a pen testing tool called "Cobalt Strike" to infiltrate target networks. MITRE reports[140] that the group APT32 is Vietnam based but its targets include other Southeast Asian countries like the Philippines, Laos, and Cambodia.

---

138 The word, "transnational" first appeared in literature in 1916 in the writings of Randolph Bourne. It latter became embedded in the field of international relations when it was used by Robert Keohane & Joseph Nye (1972). The authors used this term to describe "complex interdependence" in international relations to imply that actions and consequences by states are inextricable tied together. See Robert Keohane and Joseph Nie; "Transnational Relations and World Politics;" Harvard University Press, 1972.

139 CSIS; "Significant Cyber Incidents;" https://www.csis.org/programs/technology-policy-program/significant-cyber-incidents

140 https://attack.mitre.org/groups/G0050/

Subsequent investigations by FireEye reveal that the group's intrusions include Vietnam (2014); Germany (2014); Philippines (2016); China (2016); and United States (2016). APT32 used malware capabilities which include Windshield, Komprogo, Soundbite, Phoreal, and Beacon. The C2 (command and control) domains were registered using Privacy Guardian on August 21, 2017, and all host names resolved to the same Canadian IP address. There were other domains scattered throughout the world and included France, Germany and other nations.

Unexplored questions emerge from the above discussion: Were the different malware codes written in Vietnam or acquired from the dark web? From where? Which countries? As this exploration expands, it will most certainly bring other nation states into the incident. Few cyber incidents are contained to one nation – perhaps, the Melissa virus of 1999 was one. Analysis of the this virus is largely silent on how far outside the United States did the virus spread. The author David Smith write the malware in the United States and the virus largely used networks in the United States to affect victims in the US. Given the connectivity of machines today; it is hard to imagine a scenario where such a containment could be possible.

The reason to think in terms of globality in this context is important because if we agree that cyber crime is "global" then policy and legal discussions need to be "global" as well. It is certainly possible to prosecute cyber crime in one nation as long as a legal system exists to prosecute them. However, when these legal systems are so different as to be considered "weak;" they can support the spread of cyber crime into other nations. How then, should we think in terms of legal framework to control and mitigate cyber crime? Below I present one way to structure such an arrangement.

In this framework, a cyber perpetrator located in Nation A can commit a crime in Nation A using cyber infrastructure in the same nation. This scenario is the easiest to visualize when Country A's laws and processes can be used to prosecute the crime. Should the cyber victim be located in countries B or C or other's; then it is necessary that there be bilateral agreements by which countries can prosecute the crime and seek jurisdiction over the cyber perpetrator(s) and any evidence in the prosecution of the crime. Perhaps the most complex scenario is where a cyber perpetrator in nation A uses infrastructure in X, Y.... and other territories to commit a crime in multiple nations. It is rather difficult to envisage bilateral agreements in all pairs of states to bring this crime to justice.

The real need in cyber crime and cyber law, then, is the development of a transnational regime or a set of legal and policy arrangements which can be used to deter such acts and/or bring the crime to justice in one/ more of the nations involved. Such an arrangement is currently missing in the cyber ecosystem. Below, I discuss each of the arrangements with examples from different nations.

Cyber Perpetrator	A	A+X	A+X+Y...
Cyber Victim			
A	National Laws	National Laws	National Laws
B	Bilateral Agreement	Cyber Regimes	
C	Bilateral Agreement		

Figure 6: Legal famework to contorl and mitigate cyber crime

National Cyber Laws

Most countries today have some framework in the cyber arena. Countries base their laws on their own national requirements and the laws themselves are influenced by broad framework principles which may or may not be consistent with those in other countries. The UNCTAD reports[141] that 72% of countries have cyber legislation while 18% have none with 9% having draft legislation only. Of course, the nature of this legislation is very different, and the interpretation of laws is too.

The United States has probably the most robust and effective cyber security laws. Three main federal cybersecurity regulations govern conduct by organizations:

- 1996 Health Insurance Portability and Accountability Act (HIPAA)

- 1999 Gramm-Leach-Bliley Act

- 2002 Homeland Security Act which included the Federal Information Security Management Act (FISMA)

More recent laws have been enacted to improve the security environment and these include:

- Cybersecurity Information Sharing Act (CISA) of 2015

- Cybersecurity Enhancement Act of 2014

---

141   https://unctad.org/en/Pages/DTL/STI_and_ICTs/ ICT4D-Legislation/eCom-Cybercrime-Laws.aspx

- Federal Exchange Data Breach Notification Act of 2015

- National Cybersecurity Protection Advancement Act of 2015

- Computer Fraud and Abuse Act of 1984

There are, of course, State Cyber Security Laws such as New York and California which are designed to monitor cyber threats to financial systems, infrastructure, and information networks. California has recently[142] introduced legislation called AB 375 which is targeted at data protection and consumer privacy rights.

There have been several notorious prosecutions under the above-mentioned laws: Robert Morris (1990); David L. Smith (1999); Robert Keppel (2003); Max Butler (2008); Albert Gonzales (2008) and Kevin Mitnick (1999).

Bilateral Arrangements

Joint efforts between countries have grown in response to transitional incidents of cybercrime. Such cooperative arrangements serve to increase the reach of law enforcement in one country to individuals in other nations. This is particularly true for the United States and some examples are below.

1. Vytautas Parfionovas, 32, a Lithuanian national, was arraigned in Brooklyn federal court in

---

142 AB 375 was published on 06/29/2018. https://leginfo.legislature.ca.gov/faces/billTextClient.xhtml?bill_id=201720180AB375

November 2019, on charges of money laundering and aggravated identity theft. Prosecutors revealed that he and co-conspirators stole approx. $5.5 million by stealing passwords to brokerage accounts and making trades for their won benefits. They also stole passwords to bank accounts and sent requests to banks for overseas wire transfers. Parfionovas was arrested in Ukraine and extradited to the US.

2. Peter Levashov, 37, a Russian citizen was arrested while on holiday in Barcelona, Spain, and extradited to the United States. He had previously been charged by US prosecutors in connection with the Kelihos botnet, a network of more than 100,000 infected devices by cyber criminals to distribute viruses, ransomware, phishing emails and other spam attacks.

3. Djevair Ametovski, a Macedonian citizen, was indicted in the United States with crimes related to his operation of the web site Codeshop.su – a web site allegedly created for the sole purpose of selling illegally obtained credit and debit card data and personal information for financial gain. Ametovski was arrested in Ljubljana, Slovenia, on January 22, 2014, and was extradited to the United States.

4. In just one day in 2008, an American credit card processor (RBS WorldPay) was hacked. A team of hackers and cashers in 280 cities around the world, stole over $9 million in 12 hours from 2100 ATM's worldwide. Following an investigation by the United States, 14 individuals were charged and Evgeny Tarasovich

Levitskyy, a/k/a Vinchenco, a/k/a Vinch, a/k/a M.U.R.D.E.R.E.R., 31, of Nikolaev, Ukraine, was extradited from the Czech Republic to the United States to face charges of conspiracy to commit bank fraud and wire fraud.

5. Alex Yucel, the leader of a group called Blackshades, a citizen of Sweden, was arrested by the US in Moldova and extradited to the United States in 2015. He was charged for distributing software used to hack half a million computers worldwide.

The United States has created cyber agreements with various nations such as China to reduce incidents of cyber crime. In 2015, Obama and Xi Jingping reached an agreement pledging that there would not be government sponsored economic espionage in cyberspace. The U.S.-China Cybersecurity agreement is a bilateral agreement meant to prevent the economically motivated cyber espionage between the two countries, particularly the theft of intellectual property and trade secrets. Some of the other notable bilateral agreements are:

A. United States – Australia: The 1951 ANZUS (Australia, New Zealand, United States Security Treaty) was amended in 2011 with a clause to add cyberspace to the military defense agreement.

B. New Zealand – Australia: Australia's Counter-Terrorism and Emergency Management Committees agreed to work together in the cyber incident response areas to ensure that networks of national importance remain resilient to cyber intrusion.

C. United States – Canada: cyber security cooperation is part of the action plan <u>Beyond the Border: A Shared Vision for Perimeter Security and Economic Competitiveness</u> between the two countries.

D. United States – India: The United States and India signed a Memorandum of Understanding (MOU) today to promote closer cooperation and the timely exchange of information between the organizations of their respective governments responsible for cybersecurity.

Cyber Regimes And Why We Need Them

On July 15, 2015, Europol announced that law enforcement and judicial authorities worldwide had taken down one of the most prolific cybercriminal forums: Darkode. The operation was led by the FBI and supported by Europol's European Cybercrime Centre (EC3), with the involvement of law enforcement officers from 20 countries[143] in and outside the European Union. The takedown and arrests were coordinated from command posts set up by the FBI (Pittsburgh, USA) and Europol's EC3 (The Hague, the Netherlands). From the command post in EC3, representatives of the Republic of Srpska (Bosnia and Herzegovina), Cyprus, Denmark,

---

143 Australia, Brazil, Canada, Croatia, Colombia, Cyprus, Denmark, Finland, former Yugoslav Republic of Macedonia, Germany, Israel, Latvia, Nigeria, Republic of Srpska (Bosnia and Herzegovina), Romania, Serbia, Sweden, United Kingdom, USA. Joint action by these countries was reported by Europol Press Release: https://www.europol.europa.eu/newsroom/news/cybercriminal-darkode-forum-taken-down-through-global-action and by the US Department of Justice: https://www.fbi.gov/contact-us/field-offices/pittsburgh/news/press-releases/major-computer-hacking-forum-dismantled

Finland, Germany, Latvia, former Yugoslav Republic of Macedonia, Romania, Serbia, Sweden, United Kingdom and the FBI coordinated the technical take down of the forum, alongside further law enforcement actions, which resulted in 28 arrests, 37 house searches, and numerous seizures of computers and other equipment.

The FBI displayed the map below (Figure 7) of "Operation Shrouded Horizon" which led to the shutdown of the forum; charges filed against 12 individuals associated with the forum, including its administrator.

The more than 250-300 active users of Darkode formed a closed community. Membership was by invitation only, and after being vetted by a trusted member of the forum. Although there were several scandals, changes and rumours of the forum being compromised during the course of its existence, the Darkode forum was the place to go to if you were an English-speaking cybercriminal. The popular

Figure 7: Image from the FBI's cyber crime news website, https:// www.fbi.gov/news/stories/cyber-criminal-forum-taken-down

cybercriminal hub facilitated the trade in goods and services including malware (malicious software), Zero Day Exploits (cyber-attacks exploiting software flaws) and access to compromised servers.

The following defendants were charged in the operation:

1. Johan Anders Gudmunds, aka Mafi aka Crim aka Synthet!c, 27, of Sollebrunn, Sweden, was charged by indictment with conspiracy to commit computer fraud, conspiracy to commit wire fraud, and conspiracy to commit money laundering. He was accused of serving as the administrator of Darkode, and creating and selling malware that allowed hackers to create botnets. Gudmunds also allegedly operated his own botnet, which at times consisted of more than 50,000 computers, and used his botnet to steal data from the users of those computers on approximately 200,000,000 occasions.

2. Morgan C. Culbertson, aka Android, 20, of Pittsburgh, was charged by criminal information with conspiring to send malicious code. He was accused of designing Dendroid, a coded malware intended to remotely access, control, and steal data from Google Android cellphones. The malware was allegedly offered for sale on Darkode.

3. Eric L. Crocker, aka Phastman, 39, of Binghamton, New York, was charged by criminal information with sending spam. He was accused of being involved in a scheme involving the use of a Facebook Spreader which infected Facebook

users' computers, turning them into bots which Crocker controlled through the use of command and control servers. Crocker sold the use of this botnet to others for the purpose of sending out massive amounts of spam.

4. Naveed Ahmed, aka Nav aka semaphore, 27, of Tampa, Florida; Phillip R. Fleitz, aka Strife, 31, of Indianapolis; and Dewayne Watts, aka m3t4lh34d aka metal, 28, of Hernando, Florida, were each charged by criminal information with conspiring to send spam. They were accused of participating in a sophisticated scheme to maintain a spam botnet that utilized bulletproof servers in China to exploit vulnerable routers in third world countries, and that sent millions of electronic mail messages designed to defeat the spam filters of cellular phone providers.

5. Murtaza Saifuddin, aka rzor, 29, of Karachi, Sindh, Pakistan, was charged in an indictment with identity theft. Saifuddin is accused of attempting to transfer credit card numbers to others on Darkode.

6. Daniel Placek, aka Nocen aka Loki aka Juggernaut aka Mirror, 27, of Glendale, Wisconsin, was charged by criminal information with conspiracy to commit computer fraud. He was accused of creating the Darkode forum, and selling malware on Darkode designed to surreptitiously intercept and collect e-mail addresses and passwords from network communications.

7. Matjaz Skorjanc, aka iserdo aka serdo, 28, of Maribor, Slovenia; Florencio Carro Ruiz, aka

NeTK aka Netkairo, 36, of Vizcaya, Spain; and Mentor Leniqi, aka Iceman, 34, of Gurisnica, Slovenia, were each charged in a criminal complaint with racketeering conspiracy; conspiracy to commit wire fraud and bank fraud; conspiracy to commit computer fraud, access device fraud and extortion; and substantive computer fraud. Skorjanc also was accused of conspiring to organize the Darkode forum and of selling malware known as the ButterFly bot.

8. Rory Stephen Guidry, aka k@exploit.im, of Opelousas, Louisiana, was charged with computer fraud. He was accused of selling botnets on Darkode.

A large multinational effort was needed to bring down one of the largest English-speaking cyber crime forums. In the press release following the operation, the US Attorney David Hickton said the following: "Of the roughly 800 criminal Internet forums worldwide, Darkode represented one of the gravest threats to the integrity of data on computers in the United States and around the world and was the most sophisticated English-speaking forum for criminal computer hackers in the world. Through this operation, we have dismantled a cyber hornets' nest of criminal hackers which was believed by many, including the hackers themselves, to be impenetrable.[144]"

So powerful was this action, that other bloc's of nations started to initiate discussions about building their own version of Europol. For example, Singapore

---

144 https://www.fbi.gov/contact-us/field-offices/ pittsburgh/news/press-releases/major-computer-hacking-forum-dismantled

unveiled[145] its national plan for cyber crim which proposed a Europol-style Aseanpol to fight cyebr crime in the region. Singapore already hosts Interpol's global headquarters for cyber crime (the Interpol Global Complex for Innovation). Now it wanted to create an Asean-wide organization to combat cyber crime in Southeast Asia.

What these efforts suggest is the need for a global mechanism to influence national actions related to cyber crimes. This is precisely what a "global cyber regime" can support. In order to understand "regimes," it is necessary to look back at the evolution of international relations and organizations.

In the early 1980's, there was a marked shift in discussions related to our understanding of international relations. Previous discussions had relied more on formal organizations which have international structure and function such as the United Nations and NATO. In 1982, Steven Kasner[146] provided a first definition of regimes as "implicit or explicit principles, norms, rules and decision-making procedures around which actors' expectations converge in a given area of international relations." Regimes "are more specialized arrangements that pertain to well-defined activities, resources, or geographical areas and often involve only some subset of the members of international society." Examples of regimes include CITES (Convention on International Trade in Endangered Species of Wild Flora and Fauna), the Basel Convention which governs

---

145 https://www.computerweekly.com/news/450303321/Asean-ministers-discuss-Europol-equivalent-in-Singapore

146 Steven Krasner, "Structural causes and regime consequences: regimes as intervening variables", IO. 36,2, Spring 1982, pp. 185-205 (introduction of volume)

the international movement of hazardous waste, and the U.S.-Canada Great Lakes water quality regime. Regimes may or may not take the form of international organizations. The global nuclear regulatory regime, the International Atomic Energy Agency, does take the form of an international organization, whereas the Antarctic Treaty System that emerged in 1959 operates without any administrative apparatus. Regimes vary in other ways as well, perhaps the most significant being their degree of specificity, their geographic scope, and membership.

Regimes with information technology are dispersed across multiple issue areas.

The transnationality of information flows and impacts was first discussed in the 1970s under the rubric of the New World Information and Communication Order (NWICO) with the sole purpose to promote the democratization of information flows across countries[147]. Perhaps, the best formulation of the NWICO was presented by Mustafa Masmoudi, the Tunisian leader credited with start of the effort. He wrote[148]:

> *"Information must be understood as a social good and a cultural product, and not as a material commodity or merchandise. Seen in this perspective, all countries should enjoy the same opportunities of access to sources of information*

---

147 Many Voices One World, also know as the MacBride Report was a 1980 UNESCO Report written by Sean MacBride and was the culmination of an effort to bring communication and information flow issues to a global forum. An analysis appears at: https://www.globalpolicy.org/component/content/article/157/27023.html

148 Mustafa Masmoudi; "The New World Information Order;" Journal of Communications, June 1979.

as well as to participate in the communications process...Information is not the prerogative of a few individuals or entities that command the technical and financial means enabling them to control communications; rather, it must be conceived as a social function intrinsic to the various communities, culture, and different conceptions of civilization (1979, p. 241)."

NWICO began the advocacy of open communications, available communications channels and the unrestricted transborder data flows as a means to making information processing capabilities available to all countries. Perhaps this discussion also shaped the thought processes of Marshall McLuhan's <u>Global Village</u>[149] where he forecasted the world becoming a more interconnected place due to unrestricted information flows and media technologies propagation through-out the world.

The idealistic visions of NWICO soon ran into the reality of nationalistic ideologies such as threat to national identity due to unrestricted information flow; the reliance of economic development on information services; and economic growth based on information technology and services. Since then, the global discussion of information and information capability flow has been built on the opposing forces of a desire to have open access to information flows vs. the need as seen by nations to restrict, manage, and control information and its flow based on national needs and priorities.

It is instructive to discuss cyber security issues against this background; if only because of the fact that

---

149 Marshall McLuhan & Bruce Powers; "The Global Village;" Oxford University Press; 1992.

all cyber attacks and intrusions are a special case of transborder data flows but with a much more specific intent and purpose. Some essential pieces are in place for a global cyber regime and include the following actors and arrangements described below.

The United Nations

The UN has made efforts through its component unit – ITU (International Telecommunications Union) to secure the use of information and communications technologies. Heads of States and world leaders have entrusted ITU to be the Facilitator of Action Line C5, "Building confidence and security in the use of ICTs", in response to which ITU launched, in 2007, the Global Cybersecurity Agenda (GCA), as a framework for international cooperation in this area. In 2010 the General Assembly adopted Resolution 65/230 that proposed to establish *"an open-ended intergovernmental expert group to conduct a comprehensive study of the problem of cybercrime and responses to it by the Member States, the international community and the private sector, including the exchange of information on national legislation, best practices, technical assistance and international cooperation, with the view to examining options to strengthen existing and to propose new national and international legal or other responses to cybercrime"*[150]

The Council of Europe (Budapest Convention)

In 1997 the Council established a Committee of Experts on Crime in Cyber-space, and in 2001 the Council adopted the Convention on Cybercrime, known

---

150 Schjolberg, S., Cybercrime Law. Global organizations: ICTC (2013) http://www.cybercrimelaw.net/documents/ICTC.pdf

as the Budapest Convention. Russia objects to certain Convention provisions, which allow for what Russia considers extra-jurisdictional exercises of power that amount to interference in a country's internal affairs. Over 100 nations use the Council of Europe Convention as the basis for domestic legislation to combat the threat of cybercrime.[151] So far 35 countries are a party to the Convention.

The Organization for Economic Co-operation and Development (OECD)

The OECD established a Task Force on Spam in 2004 to address the issue of spam in developing countries[152]. The OECD Working Party on Information and Privacy (WPISP)[153] develops international guidelines on cyber security and in 2002 published a document titled "Security of Information Systems and Networks: Towards a Culture of Security." Later, in 2013, the OECD Committee on Digital Economic Policy (CDEP) agreed to revise the 2002 guidelines and in 2015 adopted the "Recommendation on Digital Security Risk Management" which replaces the 2002 Guidelines. In 2008 it also released "Scoping paper on online Identity theft" a report with some recommendations on how to fight identity theft (this document also suggested recognized identity theft as a separate offence in criminal

---

151 The Hon Nicola Roxon MP. (2012). New Laws in the Fight Against Cyber Crime http://parlinfo.aph.gov.au/parlInfo/ download/media/pressrel/1867175/upload_binary/1867175.pdf

152 Directorate for science, technology and industry committee on consumer policy committee for information, computer and communications policy. Task force on spam: spam issues in developing countries. Published may 2005..

153 The WPISP was later renamed to Working Party on Security and Privacy in the Digital Economy (SPDE).

laws.) It was followed up in 2009 by the "OECD Policy Guidance on Online Identity Theft" report[154].

The North Atlantic Treaty Organization (NATO)

In the 2002 Prague Summit, cyber defense became a part of NATO's agenda. Allied leaders reiterated the need to provide additional protection to information systems at the Riga Summit in 2006. Following the cyber attacks against Estonia's public and private institutions in 2007, Allied defense ministers agreed that urgent work was needed in this area. As a result, NATO approved its first Policy on Cyber Defense in January 2008. In the summer of 2008, the conflict between Russia and Georgia demonstrated that cyber attacks have the potential to become a major component of conventional warfare.

NATO adopted an enhanced policy and action plan, which were endorsed by Allies at the Wales Summit in September 2014. An updated action plan has since been endorsed by Allies in 2017. The policy establishes that cyber defense is part of the Alliance's core task of collective defense, confirms that international law applies in cyberspace, seeks to further develop NATO's and Allies' capabilities, and intensifies NATO's cooperation with industry. The top priority is the protection of the networks owned and operated by the Alliance.

Asia Pacific Economic Cooperation (APEC)

In 1990 APEC established its Telecommunications

---

154 Complete copies of documents are available at: https://www.oecd.org/sti/consumer/latestdocuments/6/

and Information Working Group (TEL) that works through three groups: the Liberalisation Steering Group (LSG), the ICT Development Steering Group (DSG) and the Security and Prosperity Steering Group (SPSG). Collectively these groups serve to:

1. Promote security, trust and confidence in networks and infrastructure;

2. Provide oversight of Computer Emergency Response Teams (CERTs) and Computer Security Incident Response Teams (CSIRTs);

3. Address issues of Spam, Spyware and Cybercrime prevention;

4. Oversee development of human resources and capacity in order to combat cybercrime and implement effective cyber security awareness initiatives; and

5. Facilitate partnerships with the private sector on promoting security, trust and confidence in the use of technology.

Strategic Alliance Cyber Crime Working Group (SACCWG)

SACCWG was assembled in 2006. It is a special unit consisting of five law enforcement agencies: The Australian High Tech Crime Centre (AHTCC), FBI (USA), New Zealand Police, Royal Canadian Mounted Police, and Serious Organized Crime Agency (United Kingdom). According to FBI reports[155], the group is a

---

155 https://archives.fbi.gov/archives/news/stories/2008/march/cybergroup_031708

part of the larger Strategic Alliance Group between the five countries. The following activities form the core purpose of the group:

1. Collectively develop a comprehensive overview of the transnational cyber threat—including current and emerging trends, vulnerabilities, and strategic initiatives for the working group to pursue;

2. Set up a special area on Law Enforcement Online, the FBI's secure Internet portal, to share information and intelligence;

3. Launch a series of information bulletins on emerging threats and trends (for example, how peer-to-peer, or P2P, file sharing programs can inadvertently leak vast amounts of sensitive national security, financial, medical, and other information);

4. Provide an exchange of cyber experts to serve on joint international task forces and to learn each other's investigative techniques firsthand; and

5. Share training curriculums and provide targeted training to international cyber professionals.

The above arrangement are the building blocks of a global cyber regime. It is not perfect. It represents steps by the world to stop, deter, make cyber crime more difficult and more expensive for perpetrators. The effort this takes is often extensive.

In a fascinating book, <u>Spam Nation</u>;[156] author Brian Krebs, provides meticulous details about the spam

___

156 <u>S</u>pam Nation: "The Inside Story of Organized Cybercrime-from Global Epidemic to Your Front Door;" Sourcebooks; 2014.

epidemic and the people who cause and profit from it. He notes that an average of 82,000 new malicious software variants attack our computers every day and a large percentage of these are designed to turn infected computers into spam machines – as many as 14.5 billion spam messages are generated every day. Krebs also described the "Pharma Wars;" the battle between Russian groups to sell fake pharmaceuticals via spam. It is fascinating to see the coordinated efforts of multiple groups using different laws to stop spam. These efforts (and groups) include:

1. The Federal Trade Commission (FTC) which convinced a court to stop a hosting provider called 3FN which was routing harmful content;

2. FireEye, a security firm which led an effort to bring down Mega-D botnet; leading to the arrest of Oleg Nikolaenko (the author) in Las Vegas;

3. Microsoft – which organized another effort of stop major spam botnets;

4. Arrest of 27-year old, Georgiy Avanesov in Armenia. Avanesov wrote and rented his botnet out to other spammers; and

5. The FBI, together with multiple international law enforcement partners too down the "Gameover Zeus" botnet, a collection of more than one million hacked computers.

Such global coordinated efforts can only become possible through a systematic cyber regime which reach across national boundaries and legal systems to end cyber crime which is truly global in nature. On Feb. 20, 2020, the US Justice Department unsealed indictments against four Chinese officers of the People's Liberation Army (PLA) for perpetrating the 2017 hack against Equifax which led to the theft of data of 150 million Americans. The indictments described how the men disguised their hacking activity by routing attack traffic through 34 servers located in nearly 20 countries, using encrypted communications channels within Equifax's network to blend in with normal network activity.

It is worth remembering that the Equifax breach caused the company's shares to fall 13.66% on the day the breach was announced. Equifax competitors, TransUnion and Experian) were similarly hit due to panic in the market. Consumers, of course, were the largest affected group as they were at the risk of identity theft, including names, social security numbers, birth dates, and other personal information.

It will take a lot to stop the psychological, financial, and personal harm caused by cyber weapons but the journey has begun.

www.ingramcontent.com/pod-product-compliance
Lightning Source LLC
Chambersburg PA
CBHW041636050326
40690CB00026B/5241